THE
PLOT TO KILL
LLOYD GEORGE

THE
PLOT TO KILL LLOYD GEORGE

*The Story of Alice Wheeldon
and the Pear Tree Conspiracy*

Nicola Rippon

Wharncliffe Books

First published in Great Britain in 2009 by
Wharncliffe Local History
an imprint of
Pen & Sword Books Ltd
47 Church Street
Barnsley
South Yorkshire
S70 2AS

ISBN 9 78184415 837 9

A CIP catalogue record for this book is
available from the British Library.

Typeset in Centennial by
Phoenix Typesetting, Auldgirth, Dumfriesshire

Printed and bound in England by
CPI UK

Pen & Sword Books Ltd incorporates the Imprints of Pen & Sword
Aviation, Pen & Sword Maritime, Pen & Sword Military, Wharncliffe
Local History, Pen & Sword Select, Pen & Sword Military Classics
and Leo Cooper.

For a complete list of Pen & Sword titles please contact
PEN & SWORD BOOKS LIMITED
47 Church Street, Barnsley, South Yorkshire, S70 2AS, England
E-mail: enquiries@pen-and-sword.co.uk
Website: www.pen-and-sword.co.uk

Contents

Author's Note

Evidence in the case of Alice and Hettie Wheeldon and Alf and Winnie Mason was presented over two court hearings, in Derby and in London. Written statements were also given in Derby, Southampton and at the Central Criminal Court. These sources, together with contemporary newspaper reports of the trial, have been combined to tell the story in this book. Within these sources are a number of discrepancies in the spellings of names. Wherever possible the spellings recorded on official documents have been used. Where family nicknames are used, the spellings are those that appeared in original letters.

Acknowledgements

A list of principal sources will be found at the back of this book but I would also like to acknowledge the help given by the following: Derby Local Studies Library staff; Jan Marsh, Senior Librarian (Heritage) at Bournemouth Library; Steve Roud of Croydon Local Studies Library; Carol Sklinar, who provided copies of letters sent between the Wheeldons and Lydia Robinson; Brian Reid of the Marxist Internet Archive who helped with details on Tom Bell; and, of course, my family and friends for their support and encouragement.

Nicola Rippon
Derby, Autumn 2008

List of Plates

Gavrilo Princip being taken into custody after assassinating Archduke Franz Ferdinand in Sarajevo in June 1914.

Volunteers flocking to enlist after Britain declared war on Germany in August 1914.

One of the government posters urging men to answer the call to serve King and Country.

Blinded Allied troops at a casualty clearing station on the Western Front.

Injured soldiers and their nurses at the Derbyshire Royal Infirmary in 1915.

Damage at Derby's railway works after the German Zeppelin raid on 31 January 1916.

Conscientious objectors at Dyce camp, near Aberdeen, in October 1916.

The *Daily Sketch*, 1 February 1917, reporting the first day of the sensational trial that had opened in Derby.

Alice Wheeldon's home at 12 Pear Tree Road, Derby, pictured in 2008.

Alice Wheeldon (right), Winnie Mason and Hettie Wheeldon at Derby Guildhall during the committal hearing.

Alf Mason, Winnie's husband.

Derby Guildhall.

The scene inside Derby Guildhall during the committal proceedings.

Attorney-General Sir Frederick Smith.

Arthur McManus, a vociferous anti-conscription and anti-war campaigner, who later married Hettie Wheeldon.

Tom Bell, another anti-war campaigner.

Emmeline Pankhurst being carried away from Buckingham Palace.

Imprisoned Suffragettes were force-fed by tube. Alice Wheeldon escaped this particularly unpleasant procedure.

Alex Gordon, also known as William Rickard or Francis Vivien.

Prologue

On a damp, cold day in late February 1919, twenty solemn figures gathered around an open grave on a hillside overlooking the industrial town of Derby. They had assembled to lay to rest Alice Wheeldon, mother, sister, aunt, neighbour, friend and comrade – and apparent Enemy of the State, someone who had been described as a 'desperate, dangerous person'. Among the mourners were prominent members of the pacifist movement, men and women opposed to military service, and three of the country's most notorious revolutionary Socialist activists.

A few yards away a small knot of newspaper reporters observed the grieving group. The journalists had been waiting as the four carriages of the funeral cortège pulled up outside the town's municipal cemetery. They had watched as a procession formed behind the coffin, which was borne from the hearse and through the imposing Victorian gatehouse, along a walkway to a spot not far from the grave of Alice's father. The reporters had noted with surprise that none of the mourners wore the customary black and now, as Mrs Wheeldon's 27-year-old son William stepped forward to place a carefully unfolded 'Red Flag of Socialism' on the otherwise stark oak coffin, they began to scribble furiously.

Two wreaths, one of laurel, the other of ivy and tulips, were the only other adornments. As the coffin was lowered into the ground, there was no service, no religious rites and, although Alice had at one time described herself as a Quaker, there was no mention of God, or of a higher power except that of Nature itself.

But Alice Wheeldon's passing by no means went unmarked. Stepping aside from the crowd of mourners, John S. Clarke from Jarrow, a former lion tamer, gun-runner, adventurer and revolutionary, scrambled to the top of the slippery bank. Clarke was a renowned speaker, his technique honed by years of street oration in Scotland and the North-East. Now, 'his hands upon the lapels of his fawn overcoat', he began a most remarkable valediction:

> This afternoon we are faced here with the climax of one of the world's most poignant tragedies. Don't mistake that – a tragedy. We are giving to the eternal keeping of Mother Earth, the mortal dust of a poor and innocent victim of a judicial murder. That is a frightful word to utter over the mouth of a grave, but don't mistake it, it was a murder.

In fact, like so many of those buried in the newest graves around hers, Alice Wheeldon was a victim of the influenza epidemic that had swept through Western Europe to such devastating effect since the end of the First World War. Her daughters Hettie and Winnie and her son-in-law Alf had also been struck down and remained too ill to attend the funeral. Another daughter, Nellie, was also absent, presumably too busy tending her sick siblings.

Clarke, like all those gathered, knew this and yet he re-iterated his accusations:

Incarceration in a prison, the body starved by lack of food, the mind starved by anxiety. She has returned to Nature, the Mother of us all – the victim of a cold-blooded murder. We commit her to the grave where she is beyond further torture by society. She was a Socialist and was enemy, particularly, of the deepest incarnation of inhumanity at present in Great Britain – that spirit which is incarnated in the person whose name I shall not insult the dead by mentioning. He was the one, who in the midst of high affairs of State, stepped out of his way to pursue a poor obscure family into the dungeon and into the grave.

The person in question was David Lloyd George, Britain's beloved Prime Minister, the man who had brought the nation through the most devastating war in its history.

Alice might well have been – as Clarke claimed – 'a prophet . . . of the here and now'. She might have, for 'her activities to mankind', received nothing but 'ostracism and calumny in life and a cruel end to that life'. But to the authorities she was of a 'completely diseased moral condition'. She was not only the recognised face of a movement that had been determined to undermine the war effort, but also a woman convicted, along with two members of her family, of plotting to poison the Prime Minister.

And yet there were strong doubts about the validity of that conviction, doubts that remain even ninety years after the event. Stories of fabricated evidence, suspicions of ulterior motives, allegations of political persecution have continued to proliferate. Could a government enmeshed in a terrible war and fearful of political revolution really concoct a fictitious plot to assassinate their leader in order to blame it on political enemies? Or were radical Socialists in a back-room parlour in Derby really conspiring to kill the man they blamed for an unjust war?

Chapter 1

Town at War

On 28 June 1914 the political tinderbox that was early twentieth-century Europe exploded into a full-scale conflagration. In the annexed Bosnian city of Sarajevo one Gavrilo Princip, a member of a nationalist organisation seeking Bosnian union with Serbia, drew a pistol and assassinated Archduke Franz Ferdinand, heir to the Austro-Hungarian throne. One month later Austria-Hungary declared war on Serbia. Russia mobilised troops in support of the Serbs. Then Germany, in support of its Austrian allies, declared war on Russia. German strategy called for an invasion of Russia's ally, France, through Belgium. On 4 August Britain, honouring her promise to protect Belgian neutrality, was drawn into the conflict. The First World War had begun.

The effects on Britain's civil population were felt almost immediately. In Derby, an industrial town in the East Midlands, it was announced that the price of bread had gone up by a halfpenny a loaf. Shortages of flour and sugar followed. Rationing was introduced almost at once and E.H. Simpson's, tailors of St James's Street, warned: 'Blue serges are very dear and will be more so.' And yet, as the *Derby Daily Telegraph* informed its readers darkly: 'Empire Faced with a

1

Life and Death Struggle', the initial reaction to the war was one of unbridled enthusiasm. Thousands of men immediately volunteered for the armed forces, encouraged with patriotic fervour by their countrymen and women.

On 14 August the British Expeditionary Force landed in France and set up defensive positions just over the Belgian border, near Mons. It was here, one week later, that the first British–German battle of the war took place as the British attempted to halt the German advance towards Paris. The Western Front soon widened and battles followed at the Marne, the Aisne, Antwerp and Armentières; by October fighting had begun near the Flemish town of Ypres. In February the following year British forces were sent to the Dardanelles, the straits separating the Black Sea from the Aegean. German–Austrian–Turkish control of this vital seaway, and of the Baltic Sea, had physically isolated Russia from her allies and prevented the shipping of supplies to Western Europe from the East. Attempts to reopen the straits using naval power alone failed, and Allied troops were landed in the area. The disastrous Gallipoli campaign that followed resulted in the deaths of around 44,000 Allied troops, more than 20,000 of them British.

By the end of 1914 the Western Front's system of trenches, dug-outs and barbed-wire fences stretched from the Belgian coast to the Swiss border. By the end of 1915 the British front line alone stretched for some 70 miles. The year 1916 would prove to be one of the most terrible in British military history. The fighting in France, and Flanders in particular, resulted in hundreds of thousands of dead and injured British soldiers. In the summer fighting began along the Somme. For seven days the Allies attacked a long front with heavy bombardment. Assuming the German gun emplacements would have been pulverised by the guns, British commanders sent front-line soldiers towards the German positions on 1 July. The tactics were simple: the troops were sent 'over the top' and told to walk towards the German emplacements in long, even lines.

But the British guns had proved ineffective against the German barbed wire and trenches, and row upon row of Allied soldiers were mown down by German machine-guns. German shells killed many before they even left their trenches. Almost 20,000 British soldiers were killed on the first day and more than 40,000 wounded. By the battle's conclusion in November, some 125,000 British and Empire soldiers had been killed, and another 300,000 wounded. In total more than a million men were dead or injured. Many towns, particularly in the north of England, had formed 'Pals battalions' and these had suffered terrible losses on the Somme. The dreadful cost of such battles to British morale was incalculable.

Meanwhile, German U-boats were attacking Allied vessels, including supply ships in the Atlantic, and conditions in Britain were approaching a critical stage. Further shortages were caused as Britain's factories turned over from peacetime production to munitions. Both sides of the conflict were coming to realise that unconditional victory was far from certain and, as he considered discussing peace terms with Germany, Liberal Prime Minister Herbert Asquith found his party divided. Blamed for the horrors of Gallipoli and the Somme, and for the Irish Easter Rising, Asquith found many of his party lined up behind his former Chancellor of the Exchequer, David Lloyd George, who was then Minister of Munitions in the coalition government. In July 1916 Lloyd George was appointed Secretary of State for War. Five months later, with the support of the Conservative and Labour leaders, he replaced Asquith as leader of the nation. The new Prime Minister refused absolutely to talk peace with Germany. Despite indications to the contrary, he convinced the majority of the country that Britain could prevail, no matter what.

In Derby local industry had enthusiastically turned its production towards assisting the war effort. The Carriage & Wagon Works produced ambulance trains, army wagons and parts for rifles. The neighbouring Loco Works began to turn out field-gun carriages and gun cradles, as well as recycling

18-pounder brass shell-cases. Hundreds of local women took factory jobs to replace the men who had gone to the front. Many refugees, particularly from Belgium, were cared for in Derby.

As hundreds of local men went off to war, local businesses did their best to comfort those left behind. Weston's chemist's shop in St Peter's Street wondered: 'How can your boy stand at ease if he is worried by vermin?' but promised that its 'Kergold Belt' would provide 'six months' freedom from body pests' for just 2*s* 6*d*.

The majority of Derby men who volunteered or were conscripted served with either the Sherwood Foresters or the Derbyshire Yeomanry. When war was declared the Sherwood Foresters, which had its depot at Derby's Normanton Barracks, comprised eight battalions; by the end of the war the regiment had thirty-three battalions, twenty of which served overseas. Around 140,000 men served with the Foresters between 1914 and 1918, almost all of them from Derbyshire and Nottinghamshire.

Local men had served in almost every major action of the war, including the bitter fighting on the Aisne in September 1914. The Foresters had fought in the ill-fated Gallipoli campaign and had distinguished themselves on the opening day of the Somme. On both occasions they suffered severe casualties. Altogether over 11,000 Sherwood Foresters did not return from the war, and one story perhaps sums up the plight of many of their families. In July 1915 the 10th Battalion had arrived in France and moved almost immediately into the bloody Ypres salient. In March the following year Private Thomas Brown of the 10th Battalion was killed in action during the British counter-attack on the Ypres–Comines Canal. Before he joined up, Brown, who was 39, had worked for Derby Corporation and lived at 38 Mundy Street, in Derby's West End, an area of largely poor housing. He left behind a widow, Sarah, and seven children, none of them old enough to work. Sarah Brown obtained a job at a yeast mill in Leaper

Street, working from 6am to 6pm. An unusually understanding employer let her pop back home at 8.30am to ensure that her children were all up, washed and ready for school. It seems to have been the only help she ever received.

The Derbyshire Yeomanry remained in England until April 1915 when they set sail for Egypt, from where three-quarters of the regiment were sent to the Suez Canal with the remainder being posted to Gallipoli. After incurring heavy losses the regiment was reunited in Egypt once more and in early 1916 redeployed to Salonika in Greece as part of a massive offensive against the pro-German Bulgarians.

Many Derbyshire men were recipients of gallantry medals. The first, and perhaps the most lauded, was 33-year-old Private Jacob Rivers of the Sherwood Foresters. On 28 April 1915, during fighting at Neuve Chapelle, he twice crept up on German gun emplacements and 'hurled bombs on them', causing the enemy to retreat. On the second occasion Rivers was killed. His widowed mother received his posthumous Victoria Cross from George V. A further four Derbyshire men – Fred Greaves at Passchendaele, Charles Stone and Bill Gregg in France, and Charles Hudson in Italy – were all awarded the VC before the end of hostilities.

For the people left behind in Derby the war was to come much closer to home at the end of January 1916, when a German Zeppelin dropped its bombs on the town. The Zeppelins' effectiveness in all weather conditions, in particular under cover of darkness, made them the nemesis of the fragile and flimsy British biplanes sent up to attack them. Since the first attacks in January 1915 the airships had become more and more daring, their bombing raids advancing ever north-wards. On the night of 31 January ten Zeppelins crossed the Channel and passed over Derby bound for Liverpool. A special alert was issued in the town and a blackout strictly enforced, and the Zeppelins passed over without incident. However, although no official order had been given, each individual workshop at the Loco Works and the Carriage & Wagon Works elected to turn its lights back on. Factories elsewhere in the town also began to light up. Later that night, however, one of the Zeppelins returned from the North-West still laden with bombs, having failed to reach its target. Light after light in Derby's industrial heartland was shining out like a beacon. Nine high-explosive bombs were dropped near no. 9 shed of the Loco Works, inflicting severe damage and killing three men: 32-year-old fitter William Bancroft of Strutt Street; 23-year-old Henry Hithersay of Devonshire Street; and 54-year-old engine driver James Gibbs Hardy, also of Strutt Street. Another fitter, 48-year-old Charles Henry Champion of Fleet Street, died three days later from his injuries. A further five bombs were dropped on the Carriage & Wagon Works; two high-explosive bombs and one incendiary fell near the gasworks at what is now Pride Park, landing on a coal heap but fortunately failing to ignite. Two further high-explosive bombs landed at the car-testing track at Rolls-Royce's Nightingale Road Works and on what was to become a bowling green on the corner of Osmaston Road and Bateman Street. Two more bombs, probably also aimed at Rolls-Royce, fell on open land nearby. Three more fell on the Gresham Road premises of Metallite Lamps, causing great damage but no casualties. Three incendiaries landed in the yard of Fletcher's lace factory in Osmaston Road, and four in Horton Street, one of which set fire to a house.

It was little wonder, then, that across the nation there were quiet murmurings of discontent at Britain's involvement in the war. That this should happen in Derby, a town with a long tradition of enlightened, even radical, thinking, was no surprise.

Chapter 2

Town of Radicals

The area that makes up modern Derby has been inhabited since prehistoric times. In the first century the Romans established the first formal settlement; the Saxons in the sixth century and the Vikings in the ninth moved the town closer to its current centre. Thus, Derby grew up around the lowest and safest crossing point of the River Derwent, was easily accessible from other population centres and was surrounded by a plentiful supply of raw materials: the essential ingredients to transform it into the pioneering industrial community it would become. The people of Derby are, by nature, self-effacing and largely content to take life as it comes. But when faced with perceived injustices, the otherwise unassuming townsfolk have a long and consistent heritage of radicalism, dating back even before the English Civil War. Thus it should, perhaps, have been of little surprise when this outwardly sleepy Midlands town was exposed as the source of an alleged plot to kill the Prime Minister, David Lloyd George, and one of his ministers.

At least as far back as Elizabethan times Derby had been associated with rebellion. Under Elizabeth I the Roman Catholic religion was outlawed; those who practised it were liable to arrest and even death. There were, however, plenty of people willing to disobey the law for the sake of their beliefs. The Babington family, as secret Catholics, were strong supporters of Mary, Queen of Scots, and played host to her at their town house in Derby in 1585. The following year Anthony Babington was revealed as a key conspirator in the eponymous plot to assassinate Elizabeth I and install Mary as England's new Catholic monarch.

In the years leading up to the English Civil War Derbeians again marched to their own tune. While the rest of the county took the side of the monarchy, Derby became a parliamentary stronghold. The unpopular ancient ship tax, revived by Charles I and extended from ports to inland towns, required the people of Derby to supply a ship of some 350 tons together with the wages, food and arms for a crew of 140 men. Unsurprisingly, given that the town is about as far distant from the coast as it is possible to be in England, there was great resentment both towards the King, and the man responsible for collecting the tax: the high sheriff, Sir John Gell. Derby's wealthy inhabitants refused outright to submit to the tax and Gell complained of the 'ill example that Derby is setting other towns'. But by the time the Civil War broke out in August 1642, Gell too had broken ranks with his monarch. In October he led a detachment of Lord Essex's troops into Derby to take command of the town on behalf of Parliament and established a strategic command centre at his home on Friar Gate. Eventually, in 1659, the Derbeians rebelled again, this time against the Commonwealth republic. With the dream of a tolerant and free society shattered by Oliver Cromwell's military dictatorship, even Gell now called for the restoration of the monarchy. A large protest on Nuns Green was quelled only by the threat of military intervention.

One hundred years later Derby was the scene of a protest at the plight of the poor and hungry in the so-called Millstone Riots. Terrible local wheat harvests in 1755 and 1756 had meant a shortage of flour, forcing the price of basic foodstuffs beyond the reach of many working-class families. Rumours proliferated that unscrupulous producers were mixing ground peas, beans and even plaster with the flour to make meagre supplies go further. The use of new French millstones, which ground much finer flour, only served to feed the conspiracy theories. Miners in nearby Wirksworth, who had already attacked local flour mills, smashing the millstones, now set out for Derby. The town's mayor, Robert Bakewell, himself a corn merchant, sent for a detachment of troops from Nottingham. The first encounter came at Darley Abbey, where the troops were forced to withstand a barrage of rocks and stones before firing their muskets into the air and forcing the protesting miners to retreat. The next target was Snape's Mill at Nuns Green in the centre of the town, but the miners found the owner had already removed all the millstones. The proprietor of a mill in St Michael's Lane had shown less foresight and his stones were soon smashed to pieces. The next target was the flour mill on the Holmes, an island in the middle of the Derwent. A tense stand-off between the miners and the mill-owner and his friends seemed destined to end in stalemate when military reinforcements arrived. But as darkness fell the troops withdrew, leaving the mill at the mercy of the miners. In the ensuing battle the millstones were destroyed and six men were arrested. As the soldiers took the prisoners to the town lock-up, the waiting townsfolk pelted them again, being more than sympathetic to the miners' cause. Eventually unable, or unwilling, to contain their frustration any longer, the soldiers fired into the crowd. One man was hit, falling to the ground in agony, his kneecap shattered. The following day more protesters gathered in the Market Place and the mayor was forced to enrol special constables to keep order. As darkness fell, the Riot Act was read and a curfew imposed. Disturbances continued throughout the week until the prisoners were bailed. Moved by the plight of the protesters, and by the intensity of local support, a group of wealthy Derbeians formed an association to import wheat via the Derwent, and to sell it to the poor at an affordable price. Over eight months almost 2,000 bushels were shipped in and a crisis was averted.

If further proof were needed that Derbeians from all walks of life were working towards social change, the members of the Derby Philosophical Society (DPS) surely provided it. The DPS met at the King's Head Inn in the town's Cornmarket on the first Saturday of every month. Its members were industrialists, doctors, inventors, engineers, scientists and philanthropists, most of them nonconformists or atheists, and included the extraordinary polymath Erasmus Darwin. They discussed scientific endeavour, social health care, civil rights and even the abolition of slavery. They were rebels too, because, like the members of the more famous Lunar Society – to which several DPS members also belonged – many supported both the French and American Revolutions. Even John Whitehurst, doyen of scientific instrument makers and 'grandfather of geology', a man not normally noted for his vocal radicalism, wrote in a letter to his friend Benjamin Franklin of the 'duties imposed upon the North Americans'. Two years after the British surrender in America, Whitehurst congratulated Franklin on his country's independence.

The Industrial Revolution of the late eighteenth and nineteenth centuries, and the transformation of Britain from an agrarian to an industrial society, saw the development of organised Socialism. The aristocracy, who had for centuries controlled the lives of the rest of their countrymen and women on the basis of their social position, found the 'natural order' had been disturbed as a new middle class of industrialists attained financial independence. Workers, too, wanted to make their political voices heard.

On 8 October 1831 the refusal of the Tory-dominated House of Lords to pass Lord Grey's Reform Bill caused widespread rioting across the country. Some of the most violent protests against the refusal of the Reform Bill occurred in Derby. Mass migration from the countryside to the towns in post-Industrial Revolution Britain had left many electoral wards virtually empty, save for perhaps one or two wealthy landowners, while

other heavily populated regions had no parliamentary repre-
sentation at all. The Bill, which sought to rectify this imbalance
and to raise the number of adult males eligible to vote to
include all those who owned property valued above £10, had
proved exceptionally popular and there had been widespread
celebration when it passed through the Commons.

Derby received word of the Lords' rejection by way of the
7pm mail coach. Almost immediately unrest broke out, with an
angry crowd gathering in the Market Place. The protesters
entered the town's churches and, throughout the night, rang a
funeral peal. Another mob sought out the homes and businesses of those who had spoken against the Bill. Windows of
properties in the Market Place were the first to be targeted. At
no. 14, printer and stationer William Bemrose, who had
vocally petitioned against the Bill, found his shop looted and its
contents burnt in the street outside. Although he and his wife
remained in their home throughout the riot, their 4-year-old
son was passed through a window to the safety of a neighbour's arms. Before long, thousands of protesters had filled
the streets. Mobs marched on Tory-owned properties such as
Chaddesden and Markeaton Halls, and even the pleas of
Reformist banker William Baker of Friar Gate failed to prevent
attacks on the homes of his Tory neighbours.

The following morning a public meeting in the town's
Guildhall was disrupted with demands for the release of two
protesters arrested the previous night. When this was refused
the angry mob made for the Borough Gaol in Friar Gate, where
an estimated 1,000 rioters broke into the prison using an
uprooted lamp-post as a battering ram, and released all
twenty-three prisoners. In neighbouring Vernon Street, at the
new County Gaol where more than 600 prisoners were under
lock and key, the governor, Richard Eaton, ordered armed
guards to protect the prison. His fears were well founded; his
brother Thomas had been forced to flee his house by St Mary's
Bridge in disguise after it had come under attack the previous
evening. The relentless advance of the crowd towards the gaol

caused the guards to fire towards them and four people were wounded. One was an innocent onlooker named Garner, who later died from his wounds. He was just 17 years old.

As the disorder continued into Monday, the politically driven hardcore rebels were joined by a large number of criminally minded rioters, whose sole aim seemed to be to cause as much chaos and destruction as possible. Now any house became a target, regardless of the political leanings of its occupant. The fine wrought-iron railings at All Saints' Church were damaged, windows were broken and undefended properties looted. Again tragedy struck as Henry Haden, the son of a former mayor, was attacked and killed by rioters. During a battle between protesters, who were smashing stalls in the Market Place, and the sabre-wielding 15th Hussars, another innocent man was killed as he sought shelter in the doorway of the Greyhound Inn. Eventually, after four days of mayhem, the tension subsided, but the people of Derby had made their point. Eventually a series of Reform Bills brought into law many of the provisions that the crowds had been demanding.

For many, however, the reforms did not go nearly far enough. In 1838 William Lovett drew up the so-called People's Charter, which proposed the introduction of annual general elections and secret ballots; electoral districts with equal numbers of eligible voters; an extension of voting rights to all men over the age of 21; the freedom of any man, whether a landowner or not, to become an MP; and the introduction of a wage for MPs so that those men who needed to work might also serve in Parliament. In 1848 Karl Marx and Friedrich Engels published their Communist Manifesto, putting into print for the first time the beliefs and aims of more extreme Socialism. But for most Derbeians at least, it was the everyday struggles, rather than idealism, that motivated them into action.

Electorally disenfranchised they may have been, but time after time Derby's working classes made their voices heard. In the early 1830s Derby was the location of one of the most celebrated trades union rebellions in Britain's history. A minor economic recession had hit the textile industry. To decrease production costs, many mill-owners had reduced workers' pay or taken advantage of technological advancements, allowing them to lay off many employees. As a means of protection the workers began to form small trades unions. Although such unions had been legal since 1825, membership was still considered provocative. Fearing that the unions would interfere with the smooth running of their businesses, or even challenge their authority, employers went to great lengths to persuade workers not to join. A tide of Socialism, however, was rising through the working classes and mill workers felt sure that, with so many of them joining together, their employers would be forced to listen to their concerns, grant them some measure of security, improve their working conditions and perhaps even increase their pay. But the mill-owners had no intention of bowing to what they saw as bullying and a conflict was inevitable.

It came in Derby in November 1833. Ralph Frost, a silk mill-owner, dismissed a worker who had refused to pay a fine imposed for shoddy workmanship. Immediately his colleagues walked out in protest. The unions rallied to the cause and silk workers all across Derby joined the spontaneous strike. It was the first encounter in a long battle of strength between employer and employee.

Concerned that the dispute was spiralling out of control, the mill and factory owners met at the King's Head and resolved to prevent any escalation. Naively they believed that if they refused to employ any worker who was part of a union, then the workforce would back down and conflict could thus be avoided. In fact, this approach served only to make matters worse. With production at a standstill, several owners brought in workers from outside the area. The unions labelled the incomers 'Black Sheep' and they and their families were subjected to verbal and sometimes physical abuse. There were countless arrests, mostly of strikers who had simply insulted or mocked their rivals. One man, Thomas Mead, was imprisoned for three months for trying to persuade another mill worker to join the strike. There were dozens of violent incidents, including one in February 1834 when an attempt by some Black Sheep to avenge the abuse of one of their colleagues resulted in the stabbing of Joshua Brown, who was not even a member of the union and was standing in his own doorway simply observing the scene when he was assaulted. His attacker was sentenced to death, but this was commuted to transportation for life.

Some Black Sheep could stand the abuse no longer. One said later: 'When we arrived at Derby, Lord, how ashamed I was! We were hooted and hissed at by the women and children at the entrance to the factory in a dreadful manner . . . We were locked in night and day like prisoners on board a hulk . . .'. Eventually he and a colleague climbed over a wall and escaped back to London.

In March 1834 the strike pay of 7s per week ran out and by April most of the strikers had little alternative but to ask to be reinstated. Some 600 of them found their jobs gone and the trouble rumbled on. As late as June a strike-breaker who had been in Derby for only a week was brutally assaulted near Kedleston Street. Soon, however, a bill was passed through Parliament confirming the right of workers to form trades unions and the 'Derby Silk Mill Lock Out' entered the annals of trades union folklore, celebrated to this day by an annual parade.

Social welfare was also uppermost in the minds of many Derbeians. In 1848 twelve members of the Carpenters' & Joiners' Society formed what would become the Derby Co-operative Provident Society, which was a more politically motivated organisation than it might at first appear. Buying goods at wholesale cost, it sold them on to union members at a low price, passing all profits on to its members. It closely followed the ideals laid out by the 'Rochdale Pioneers', and was only the second such society in the world. Initially operating from a hayloft in the George Yard off Sadler Gate, it proved a roaring success and eight years later moved into bigger premises in Victoria Street. In 1859 it began to accept members from outside the union and by 1860 had forty members. By 1900 some sixty separate stores and departments were running under its control.

The Fabian Society, which had been established as a Socialist debating group, had begun lobbying Parliament for social changes. These included a minimum wage in 1906, publicly funded health care in 1911 and, during the First World War, the abolition of hereditary peerages. In 1890 Henry Hunt Hutchinson, a retired clerk to the Derby Justices, joined the society. His generosity to the cause became immediately apparent in the form of an annual donation of £200 for the funding of lectures across the country. Upon his death in 1894, Fabian leaders were surprised to learn that Hutchinson had left the residue of his estate, worth between £10,000 and £20,000, to the Fabians for 'propaganda and other purposes of the said Society and its Socialism and towards advancing its object in any way they deem advisable'. The money was put towards the establishment of a new university in London – the London School of Economics and Political Science – because, according to Fabian Edward Pease, 'a thorough knowledge of these sciences was a necessity for people concerned in social reconstruction, if that reconstruction was to be carried out with prudence and wisdom'.

The spectrum of Socialism in Britain, and in Derby in particular, was broad and of many hues. From Christian Socialist, through the Fabians and trades unionists to the Marxists, the concept of Socialism was many and varied, and yet its disparate groups joined together, finding common ground, even if it was only that they were not the capitalist establishment. Most of these groups came together in Keir Hardie's Labour Representative Committee (LRC).

In Derby, by the turn of the twentieth century, the foundations were being laid for an attempt to elect a Socialist

Member of Parliament. The LRC put up fifteen candidates in the 1900 General Election. Hardie himself stood for Merthyr Tydfil, and for Derby the committee chose Merthyr-born Richard Bell. A dedicated union man, Bell was the former organising secretary and serving general secretary of the Amalgamated Society of Railway Servants (ASRS). His candidacy in such a strong railway town as Derby was undoubtedly an astute tactic. The previous year Bell had been announced as the Derby Trades Council (DTC) candidate, only for his union to oppose it on the grounds that Bell had connections to the Liberal Party and that approved candidates should have no connection with either of the two major parties. In an attempt to change people's minds the DTC held a meeting at Derby's Temperance Hall at which Bell expressed his disappointment and pointed out that one of his union's branch secretaries was a Tory, the other a Liberal. Remarkably perhaps, both supported Bell's candidature. After the LRC meeting, at which the ASRS had been represented by Bell himself, his nomination was approved. Bell and Hardie were the only two Labour candidates elected.

At the 1906 General Election the Labour Representative Committee won twenty-nine seats although Bell, who disagreed with several key Labour policies, then stood as a 'Lib-Lab' in Derby. He resigned from Parliament in 1910, to be replaced as MP for Derby by another Welsh-born railwayman, Jimmy Thomas.

The more radical form of Socialism was finding a niche in the town, too. And four of the major figures in Scotland's burgeoning Communist movement were to have an impact in Derby, and more directly on the lives of the Wheeldon family of the Pear Tree district in the town. Arthur McManus, Tom Bell, John S. Clarke and Willie Paul were founder members of the Socialist Labour Party (SLP), which was primarily a Scottish organisation with small groups in Sheffield and Derby. The four were joint editors of the organisation's journal *The Socialist*.

As union officials, McManus, Bell and Paul had been involved in the Clydesbank Singer sewing machine factory dispute of 1911, in which 10,000 workers had come out on strike in support of twelve female colleagues who were protesting against their employer's attempt to lengthen their working hours while at the same time decreasing their pay. After repeated threats to move production elsewhere, and suggestions that those who continued to strike would not be able to find work anywhere else, Singers broke the strike in just three weeks. Around 500 employees deemed to be ring-leaders were dismissed, among them Paul and McManus.

The men were now also vocal in the anti-war movement, although Clarke was not a pacifist, believing that the only armed struggle should be between the world's working classes and their capitalist employers. In December 1915 McManus spoke at an anti-conscription rally in George Square, Glasgow. All the speakers were arrested on public order offences but, there being no disturbances at the rally and no law to prohibit voicing a personal opinion, the authorities found it impossible to lay charges against them and they were quickly released. Three months later McManus, as a member of the Clyde Workers' Committee (CWC), became involved in a dispute at Beardmores munitions works in Parkhead, Glasgow. Trouble had quickly escalated after a manager refused a shop steward access to the new female employees who had been brought in to replace workers called up for military service. Soon several factories and works across the area had gone out on strike. The government claimed that the strike was simply a ploy by the CWC to prevent the manufacture of munitions and thus harm the war effort. McManus and four other officials were deported to Edinburgh under military orders.

As nominal national leader of the fledgling shop stewards' movement, McManus was not about to let a legal restraint keep him from his union work. He regularly travelled, covertly, between several of Britain's industrial towns and cities, including Derby, to where Willie Paul had moved in 1911.

Born in Glasgow, and in his mid-30s by the time he settled in the village of Littleover to the south-west of the town, Paul ran a business in Derby that was officially a hosiery and drapery stall, but which was sufficiently profitable for him to devote a good deal of his time to spreading the Communist word. By 1915 his business was apparently so successful that Paul was able to run stalls at nos 34, 35, 36, 63–64 and 85 Market Hall. In 1917 and 1918 he organised 'social science' classes in Derby that were, by all accounts, well attended. Through these, and market stalls in Derby, Chesterfield, Manchester, Birmingham, Sheffield and Rotherham, Paul was able to surreptitiously distribute radical literature. Doubtless this would have included publications like J. O'Connor Kessack's *The Capitalist Wilderness and the Way Out*, published by the Glasgow Clarion Scouts; and the Independent Labour Party (ILP)'s brochure *Karl Marx and Modern Socialism* by Dr Eden Paul. Two further titles, and part of an ILP anti-war series, were *Militarism* and *The Peril of Conscription*, both by J. Bruce Glasier.

John S. Clarke, too, was now living in Derby. Born in Jarrow of gypsy stock, Clarke had already enjoyed a remarkable and varied life. His family were circus folk going back several generations. Receiving little formal education, Clarke was instead trained in the ways of performance and he could ride a horse bareback by the age of 10. Opting initially for a life at sea, by the age of 17 Clarke was back at the circus – this time as the 'youngest lion tamer in Britain'. He joined the Socialist cause as a young man and helped to smuggle arms to would-be revolutionaries in Russia.

Realising that he, too, must go on the run, Clarke had taken important SLP papers and other documents that the authorities might find incriminating, placed them in a metal trunk and buried them in a field outside Edinburgh, before going into hiding. With Paul already living there, and McManus a regular visitor to the town, Derby was the obvious location for his self-imposed exile.

The government had already tried to close down *The Socialist* by dismantling the presses and attempting to arrest the contributors. With two of its editors living in the area, production was moved to Derby. Remarkably, they were able to distribute an issue a month for the entire duration of the war. During that time circulation of *The Socialist* rose from a mere 3,000 copies to a staggering 20,000.

Although some of the leaders of the British Socialist movement had gone into hiding, their supporters continued to be both visible and vocal. One such man was Vale Rawlings, a founder member of the Burton upon Trent branch of the Workers' Union, and a member of the ILP since the age of 17. In June 1914 the Derby firm of F.W. Hampshire's set up a branch in Mosley Street, Burton, to manufacture flypaper. Within a week there was industrial unrest as the girls who were employed to paste the tops on to the flypaper went on strike, complaining that they could earn no more than 3*s* 9*d* for a 55-hour week, whereas girls at the Derby factory earned more. Hampshire's argued that it was all a matter of skill; if the Burton girls were as competent as their Derby counterparts, then they could earn up to 8*s* 2*d*. In his capacity as a union official, Rawlings visited the factory and talked to some of the strikers on the pavement outside. Shortly afterwards he was arrested and charged with assaulting a police inspector.

On 19 June Rawlings was brought before Burton magistrates, where a second charge, of assaulting a girl employee named Alice Horton, was made against him. A police constable told the court he had heard another union official tell Rawlings that the inspector had called him 'an undersized rat'. Rawlings replied: 'Yes, had he not done that, then I wouldn't have gone for him.'

Despite the fact that Rawlings brought six witnesses for his defence, and despite Alice Horton telling the magistrates that she had not been assaulted, rather that Hampshire's had ordered her to bring the prosecution, he was found guilty. Before being sentenced, Rawlings pointed out that he stood only 4ft 11ins tall and weighed less than 8 stone, while

Inspector Oulton was a good foot taller and twice as heavy. It was laughable, he said, that he would attempt to assault such a figure. The magistrates were not impressed by the argument and fined Rawlings 10*s* with 18*s* 6*d* costs for assaulting Inspector Oulton, and a 5*s* fine for assaulting Alice Horton, with 20*s* 6*d* costs.

Rawlings refused to pay. The alternative, he was told, was a total of twenty-one days in prison. Rawlings opted for prison and was taken from the court and driven to Derby to begin his sentence. The uproar in the Labour movement was immediate. Keir Hardie led a deputation of MPs to see the Home Secretary, Reginald McKenna, and a petition was raised demanding a retrial. On 27 June Hardie addressed a mass demonstration in Burton, and the following day a huge crowd gathered in the open space outside Derby prison in Vernon Street. At one point the singing of the Socialist anthem, the 'Red Flag' could be heard a mile away. Eventually, after much debate, Rawlings was released.

By the outbreak of the First World War the growing Socialist movement was far from the slight irritation it had once been to the authorities. Its campaigns for populist issues, and more importantly its opposition to the war, made it too divisive to ignore. And in few places was the dissent more troubling than in Derby.

Chapter 3

'Mad Women'

One of the most contentious issues of the early twentieth century was that of a woman's right to vote. For a long time there had been various small organisations devoted to the introduction of female suffrage, but they had failed to garner much public attention either in support of or against the movement. In 1897 Millicent Fawcett, the 50-year-old widow of radical Liberal MP Henry Fawcett, sister of Elizabeth Garrett Anderson (the first official female doctor in Britain) and something of a women's rights activist, founded the National Union of Women's Suffrage Societies (NUWSS), aimed at uniting the many very disparate groups in a common goal. To those who thought that women were not capable of understanding the parliamentary system, Fawcett argued that a great many women sat on school boards, and ran large estates employing servants and workers less educated than themselves but none the less entitled to vote. She also noted that since women were expected to obey the law and pay taxes, they ought to have a say in what those laws were and how that tax was spent.

Gradually, Fawcett's thoughtful, peaceful tactics were changing minds and attracting support. The NUWSS was widely supported with an estimated 100,000 members. Although none of the projected parliamentary Bills to give women the vote had actually passed through the Commons, they had attracted a great deal of support and many Suffragists felt that it was only a matter of time.

But for the well-to-do Emmeline Pankhurst and her daughters Christabel and Sylvia change was not happening soon enough. In 1903 they founded the Women's Social and Political Union (WSPU), soon adopting the *Daily Mail*'s mocking nickname 'Suffragettes'. Their motto, 'Deeds not Words', was a foretaste of their increasingly militant tactics. Although initially the WSPU confined its activities to disrupting public meetings, when this failed to attract the appropriate publicity they advanced to chaining themselves to railings and breaking windows. Those arrested found going on hunger strike an effective tactic, but the government countered this by introducing the Prisoners (Temporary Discharge for Ill-Health) Act which allowed the release of hunger-striking women and their rearrest once fit again. Some Suffragettes were repeatedly imprisoned, went on hunger strike, were released and then rearrested, hence the nickname the 'Cat and Mouse Act'.

While Fawcett and her supporters continued, slowly though it might have seemed, to increase support for their cause – their contribution to women's rights is now largely overlooked – the Suffragettes stepped up the militancy of their campaign. But acts of criminal damage – slogans painted on seats at Hampstead Heath, railway carriages slashed, golf-course grass attacked with acid, telephone wires cut and fuse-boxes forcibly blown – served only to illustrate the counter-argument that women were too unbalanced and emotional to be allowed a vote. In 1913 one of the most prominent Suffragettes, Emily Davison, attempted to seize the reins of the King's horse Anmer during the running of the Derby at Epsom. She suffered horrific injuries that claimed her life some four days later. Her fellow Suffragettes, though shocked by her death, hailed her a martyr to the cause. When Suffragettes planted bombs near the Bank of England, at Oxted station and at the under-construction house of David Lloyd George in Walton-on-the-Hill, they left no one in any doubt that they had become radical, militant and dangerous. They had ceased to be a silly irritation and were now regarded with the same fear and suspicion that might today be afforded animal rights activists, anti-globalisation protesters and even terrorists.

And there were many who agreed with the words of Lord Curzon when he claimed that the Suffragettes 'have rendered us the service of showing how easily disturbed the mental balance of some women, at any rate, can be'. Curzon, former Viceroy of India and resident of Kedleston Hall, a few miles outside Derby, was a staunch anti-Suffragist who, throughout his life, would continue to oppose women's rights.

There were, however, plenty of others in Derbyshire who did support the Suffragettes. Local membership of the NUWSS had almost doubled by the beginning of the First World War. Throughout the county at least one paid organiser was active, and through its association with the Labour movement and the TUC the NUWSS had popular support among women and men. In July 1913, during a peaceful march from Newcastle to London, a large crowd gathered in Chesterfield Market Place to hear Millicent Fawcett, Norma Smith (the NUWSS leader for Derby) and the Socialist Edward Carpenter speak. In Derby the local Trades Council also lent its support.

At the outbreak of the First World War Emmeline and Christabel Pankhurst called a halt to their organisation's violent actions, on the grounds that it would be unpatriotic to disrupt the country at so critical a time. Sylvia, however, was not so inclined and spoke out vehemently against the war. The WSPU was split in two.

In November 1909 Christabel Pankhurst had spoken at the Drill Hall in Derby. There were violent scenes as several angry men invaded the platform. Christabel, however, was unbowed, returning to the town twice in the following few weeks, each time finding less and less resistance to her cause. The following April Emmeline Pankhurst was able to hold a peaceful meeting at the same venue.

Yet there was still influential opposition. The *Derby Daily Express*, in particular, was strictly opposed to the cause, urging the 'shaving of the heads of every militant Suffragette'. It was a stance that an increasing number of local people were to take. In 1911 Edward Mundy of Shipley Hall, 11 miles from Derby, had a 300-yard-long wall erected around his property to protect it from what he saw as the Suffragette threat, and in time almost every otherwise unattributed act of violence or vandalism was blamed on the Suffragettes. One incident in particular would stain the Suffragettes' cause for some time to come.

On the night of 5 June 1914 the 900-year-old church of All Saints at Breadsall, just to the north of Derby, was set alight. According to the *Derby Daily Telegraph*, Mr Hopkins, a local farm labourer, was first to raise the alarm. Seeing a flickering glow coming from within the church, he hurried to wake the verger, Frederick Endsor, who also served as village postmaster. By the time these men, along with the Revd John Whitaker, rector of All Saints, and two churchwardens, Colonel W. Beadon Woodforde and Mr H. Buckingham, had reached the church it was fully ablaze. The fire had already outgrown any desperate attempt to douse it with buckets of water.

Because the nearest motorised fire engine was in Derby, permission to call it had first to be sought from the chairman of the local Watch Committee. By the time the engine arrived, the church was engulfed in flames and there was little that the firefighters could do, but they saved the tower and spire. As the Archdeacon of Derby examined the still-smouldering ruins, blame was already being assigned. According to the vicar of All Saints there was only one group of suspects. The Revd Whitaker told a *Derby Daily Telegraph* reporter: 'It has been done by Suffragettes, I know it has.' Suffragettes, he added, were 'mad women'.

   With few clues – any conclusive physical evidence there might have been was probably destroyed in the inferno – the authorities had little to counter or support the claims of the villagers that Suffragettes had been responsible. There was, however, little doubt that the church had been the victim of one or more arsonists. An accident was unlikely since there was no electricity or gas supply to malfunction and the church had not been open for a service that day. Nor had the heating system been used for several weeks. The fire had also spread with unexpected speed. Witnesses described a series of small explosions from inside, as if 'a trail was laid'. The villagers claimed that the fire must have been an act of revenge for a Suffragette meeting in the village having been broken up some time earlier. However, when Suffragettes had set light to churches elsewhere, a note claiming responsibility had generally been left at the scene. No such note was found at Breadsall.

   In the Revd Whitaker's newspaper interview, he challenged the perpetrators to contact him: 'I quite expect that I or one of the churchwardens will receive a message from them exulting over their wicked act.'

   Sure enough, a few days later, a card arrived. It bore the words 'Let there be light. The price of liberty. Votes for Women', and was accompanied for good measure by a page from *The Suffragette* publication. This might well have been confirmation that the Suffragettes were responsible for the fire, but it could just have easily have been sent by an opponent of women's suffrage, hoping to stir up further opposition.

   In the days after the fire, the 'case' against the Suffragettes grew steadily, built largely on circumstantial evidence and casual rumour. The only piece of possible hard evidence at the church itself was the discovery of a hatpin close to a window through which it was assumed the arsonist had gained access. The hole in the window was quite small and adjudged particularly suitable for use by a woman. That a parishioner might have innocently lost the hatpin was not given much consideration.

There were also various witness accounts of people loitering in the churchyard, but the details varied so greatly they were rendered useless. The only direct link to the Suffragettes were the words 'Votes for Women' chalked on a wall a mile away on Mansfield Road, and such political graffiti was hardly unusual. No local groups admitted, or even hinted at, responsibility. Madeline Onslow, of the Derby NUWSS, strenuously denied her organisation's involvement but the uproar died down only upon the outbreak of war.

Chapter 4

'Conchies'

After war was declared there had been an outpouring of patriotic fervour. Hundreds of thousands of men had joined up in the first few weeks of the conflict. But as time wore on, and more and more families received word of loved ones killed or horribly injured, the lines of volunteers began to shorten. In 1915 Lord Derby, Director General of Recruitment, established a scheme to encourage young men to register as volunteers, promising that they would be called up only when necessary and in strict order according to their age and marital status.

Posters encouraging Britain's young men to take up arms were displayed countrywide. Some featured bucolic images of thatched cottages and wheat fields and bore slogans such as 'Your Country's Call – Isn't this worth fighting for?' Others targeted 'the Young Women of London' and asked:

> Is your 'Best Boy' wearing Khaki? If not don't YOU THINK he should be? If he does not think that you and your country are worth fighting for – do you think he is worthy of you? If your young man neglects his duty to his King and Country, the time may come when he will neglect you.

But even such emotive propaganda proved ineffective and Prime Minister Asquith and his Minister of Munitions, David Lloyd George, began to prepare for the introduction of compulsory military service.

The ILP claimed that conscription was an infringement of basic civil liberties and groups like the No Conscription Fellowship (NCF) were established to campaign against its introduction. The NCF was the brainchild of the journalist Fenner Brockway and his wife Lilla, who ran the fledgling organisation from their Derbyshire cottage before relocating to London. At its peak the NCF boasted some 10,000 members. Its position was clear; one pamphlet declared: 'We believe in human brotherhood. In the sanctity of human life and personality. We will not kill.'

In January and May 1916 two Military Service Acts were passed, bringing conscription into law. Under the Acts every British male between the ages of 19 and 40 who was normally resident in Great Britain and who was also unmarried, or a widower without dependent children, could be called up. There were some exceptions and those excused included men who were in Britain only for education or 'some other special purpose', men in holy orders, ministers of any religious denomination, and men who had either been pensioned out of the services on health grounds or who had already been rejected for military service. Within months, however, the exemption for married men was rescinded and those previously invalided out or declared unfit had to be re-evaluated. Any man of the right age who had been resident in Britain since the outbreak of the war was now to be called up, except those who had previously been prisoners-of-war. Each man was allocated a class according to his age. Public proclamations were posted advising each class when they might expect to be called up.

A system of tribunals and appeals was established for those wishing to be given special exemption. An appellant might, for example, be successful 'if it is expedient in the national interests that he should be engaged in other work, or if he is being educated or trained for any other work', and 'that he should continue . . . if serious hardship would ensue owing to his exceptional financial or business obligations or domestic position'.

Some objected to military service on moral grounds and were termed 'conscientious objectors'. They generally fell into two categories: those who opposed this particular war on political grounds, whose appeals would almost certainly be denied; and those who objected to all wars, such as pacifists, Christadelphians and Quakers. Even their applications were usually refused outright. Those individuals still refusing to serve once the tribunal had ruled against them were court-martialled and sentenced to prison terms. Those whose appeals were successful were required to perform non-combatant war work. Many became stretcher-bearers on the battlefields, never taking up arms, but willing to put themselves in harm's way to help those who did. Some worked in military logistics, in factories doing vital war work, or in agriculture. But for many COs, the 'Absolutists', the idea of contributing in any way to the war effort was unthinkable. Some 1,500 of the 16,500 COs granted temporary or permanent exemption fell into this category and were compulsorily enlisted. When they refused to report for duty, they were arrested and imprisoned. Only 350 applicants were granted unconditional exemption.

The social stigma of being a 'conchie' cannot be over-estimated. COs faced ostracism and accusations of cowardice, sometimes even physical violence, particularly at the hands of those whose loved ones were in the thick of the fighting. In Cardiff in November 1916, where anti-pacifist posters had been displayed around the city warning against 'false peace agitators', a meeting of the National Council for Civil Liberties, with speakers like Derby MP Jimmy Thomas and Ramsay MacDonald, who had resigned as Labour leader in protest at the war, was disrupted by protesters who had gathered at

Cardiff City Hall to participate in a 'monster open-air demonstration and procession'.

Many COs, their appeals rejected or the terms of their exemption unacceptable to them, went on the run. The NCF kept detailed records of every tribunal, appeal, court martial and imprisonment. Its members visited those interned and often picketed prisons. Details of individual cases were published in the NCF's journal *The Tribunal*. But the NCF also worked underground, establishing a secret network of safe houses where on-the-run COs could hide. Its members also helped many men to escape the country entirely.

In Derby so many local men lodged appeals that tribunals were heard daily at the Town Clerk's office in Tenant Street. Derby Town Council appointed the same men who had sat on its Derby Scheme panel: the mayor, Alderman Albert Green, Alderman William Hart and councillors Arthur Longdon, Dr Robert Laurie, Henry Surtees and Walter Raynes. However, Raynes, the only Labour councillor on the committee, was a vocal opponent of conscription and refused to participate, telling his colleagues: 'Were I of military age, I should possibly have to do something to oppose the law.'

The problem with local tribunals, of course, was that what might be admissible in one jurisdiction might not in another, and members were sometimes inclined to pass judgement based on their own prejudices and interests. In Derby, cases were given short shrift. In April 1916 A.L. Smart, Derby secretary of the NCF, wrote to the *Derby Daily Telegraph*, expressing his disgust at the way the tribunals were being conducted:

> Many of us had qualms about appearing before these tribunals because we felt that no body of men, much less a body consisting of militarists and capitalists, could satisfactorily decide as to whether we had a conscientious objection . . . On Monday, five conscientious objectors were refused in the space of three

minutes. How can any tribunal ascertain whether an applicant is sincere in 36 seconds?

The Derby tribunal ruled that a member of the Church of England was allowed to register for non-combatant duties only, while members of the ILP were all marked for combatant service.

In July 1916 Mayor Albert Green himself was called up but, as the *Derby Daily Telegraph* reported, he need not have worried because he was 42. Green had registered under the Derby Scheme, safe in the knowledge that he would soon be too old to be considered. And if the age group should be extended, the newspaper told its readers that Green would still be safe because he already held a badge issued by the Ministry of Munitions, excusing him from military service because of the 'numerous and important war contracts he had undertaken'.

An Abbotsholme schoolteacher appealed on the grounds that, as a teacher of modern languages, he was indispensable. When the tribunal heard that his father was German by birth, albeit a naturalised British subject, his appeal was turned down, as was that of the manager of a sanitary pottery works in Swadlincote. Aged 23 and newly married, he claimed that his company was now engaged on essential war work and, out of an original workforce of thirty, only twenty-one men remained. He was granted a two-month delay while his employers found another manager. Meanwhile, a local tradesman who was appealing on behalf of one of his workers pointed out that not only did he himself have a son serving in the Army, but that several of his employees had joined the services; moreover, he had tried to make good soldiers out of them by rigging up a shooting range in his works yard, to help his men practise shooting Germans.

Those giving moral objections fared little better. Several members of the Church of God explained that they could not fight for religious reasons. One of them, an employee of the Great Northern Railway Company, told his hearing that, if he saw a German 'outraging his sister' he would try to get her away.

'But if you could not do so without striking a blow, would you hit the German?' the chairman asked.

'No.'

'What should you do, then?'

'I should trust in the living God.'

'I'm very glad I'm not your sister,' the chairman told him, dismissing his appeal.

The majority of the members of the public in Derby were no more understanding. In May the Derby NCF held a public meeting at the Unity Hall, at the junction of Normanton Road and Burton Road. The organisers, expecting a large turn-out, made arrangements for an overflow meeting to be held. They were to be disappointed. Even the main venue was half-empty. By then, the first prosecutions of men who had failed to report for military service had begun. In courts martial held at Normanton Barracks, the depot of the Sherwood Foresters, several COs were each sentenced to 56 days' detention. All this was against a background of daily reports in the newspapers listing Derbyshire men killed or wounded, or occasionally being awarded medals for gallantry, but the papers also reported cases where soldiers, several of them from the Sherwood Foresters, were being tried for desertion.

In July 1916 Alexander Mann Macdonald appeared before a court martial at Normanton Barracks accused of refusing to sign his record of service papers. Macdonald, who was described as an insurance agent of Cheviot Street in Derby, had not disputed the allegation; just the opposite, in fact. He had told the court that militarism was detrimental to the people of all lands insofar as it existed solely for the purpose of maintaining the power of the capitalists. He had not appeared before the local tribunal at Derby because its members had shown a poor idea of justice to conscientious objectors. He was, he claimed, a member of an international organisation for whom he had lectured as a Socialist and antimilitarist before and during the present war. Some time after this Macdonald went on the run, determined to avoid both military service and imprisonment. He took refuge in a local safe house: the home of Mrs Alice Wheeldon of Pear Tree Road, Derby.

Alice and her daughter Hettie had helped countless COs escape the attentions of the authorities. Among them was John S. Clarke, the SLP activist, who spent most of the war hiding at Mr Turner's farm at Arleston, now part of Sinfin on the southern outskirts of the town. Others were billeted around the town in Derby's secret network of safe houses.

Chapter 5

The Wheeldons

For a woman who would find herself catapulted into international notoriety, Alice Wheeldon's early life was largely uneventful. She was born Alice Ann Marshall on 27 January 1866, at 5 Russell Street, Derby, the daughter of Ann and William Marshall. Her father, like so many of his neighbours in the railway suburb of Litchurch, worked in the local engineering industry. Alice was the fifth of six children. She had three older brothers, Charles, Thomas and James; an older sister Mary; and one younger sibling Ellen. The peripatetic nature of William Marshall's job led the family to travel extensively through the industrial north of England. Their first move, however, was a few doors away, to 47 Russell Street, where they are listed on the 1871 census. Ten years later the now-widowed William was working as an engine driver and living at Broad Cut, near Horbury, just outside Wakefield. Mary was married but still lived in the family home with her baby son, James Scargill. Ellen was still at school, but 15-year-old Alice was working as a domestic servant.

In 1886 Alice married William Augustus Wheeldon, a widowed engine fitter some fourteen years her senior, at the Register Office in West Derby, Lancashire. They were already living in the same house: 51 Rimrose Road, Bootle. Quite how, or where, the couple met is unclear. Perhaps he was particularly attracted to her Derby origins, for William Wheeldon had been born and raised in the Abbey Street area of the town. His early childhood was spent just around the corner in Wilson Street and as a young man he had lived nearby at 166 Gerard Street, with his parents, William and Harriet. His father worked as a mechanical engineer, and from an early age William junior had found work in the same industry. His sisters Emma and Harriet were older than he, with Harriet employed as a day-school governess.

William Wheeldon's first wife of twelve years, Rosamund Newton, the daughter of a Derby tailor named Isaac, had died of heart failure in 1885, leaving William to take care of their two daughters Lily and Mabel at their home at 117 Abbey Street, shop premises next to the Vine Inn; William now described his occupation as that of 'botanist'.

After William and Alice married, he found work as a commercial traveller and on 1 December 1888 their first child, Nellie, was born at 87 Marsh Lane, Bootle. A second daughter, Harriett Ann, always known as Hettie, was born a little over two years later, on 25 February 1891; and on 21 January 1892 a son, William Marshall, was born. A family move to Blackburn came just months before the birth of their youngest child, Winnie, at 7 Alexandra Road on 13 December 1893.

Despite their lives now being centred on the North-West, the Wheeldons retained their Derby connections. Alice's father, William Marshall, had re-established himself in Derby by 1891. He ran an off-licence at 161 Pear Tree Road, and also worked as a travelling salesman for the nearby Offiler's brewery. His 25-year-old daughter Ellen assisted him. Alice's father was to die in May 1898. William Wheeldon's eldest children, Lilly and Mabel, were also living in Derby, at the home of their two aunts, Emma and Harriet, on Burton Road, just a few hundred yards from the home they had once shared with their parents.

By 1901 William and Alice Wheeldon had returned to Derby with their young family. The census for that year records them living at 91 Stanhope Street, just around the corner from Alice's younger sister Ellen, who had set up home with her husband William Land at 54 Pear Tree Road. By 1914 Ellen, now apparently separated from her husband, was living at 102 Pear Tree Road, a house associated with the no. 1 stable yard of Offiler's, for whom she worked as a commercial representative.

Although William Wheeldon was still listed as a commercial traveller, he was unemployed at this time. Nellie, Harriett and William junior were all at home on the night of the 1901 census, but not the unfortunate 7-year-old Winnie, who found herself a patient at the Borough Isolation Hospital, which lay between Derby and Breadsall. Alice's stepdaughters, Mabel and Lily, now in adulthood, were also living in Derby. Mabel still lived with her Wheeldon aunts, while Lilly had married window cleaner John Vernon and lived with her in-laws, Snowden and Mary Vernon, at 2 Stockbrook Street close to the town centre.

By the outbreak of the First World War the Wheeldons had a home on London Road and Alice's shop at 12 Pear Tree Road. According to the *Derby & District Directory* of 1915–16, Mrs Alice Wheeldon is recorded as a 'wardrobe dealer': that is, she bought and sold the contents of people's wardrobes. Anecdotal evidence suggests that William and Alice's marriage was not without its problems. There were suggestions that William was too fond of alcohol, and that it unleashed in him a particularly unpleasant, even violent, streak. His work certainly took him away from the family home for long periods, although it is clear that the couple remained in regular contact: his Post Office bank book was kept at Alice's home along with those of other family members. Other accounts claim that marital problems arose due to Alice's increasingly militant political beliefs.

Alice Wheeldon had become well known in Derby for her

passionate Socialism and her fervent support for the Suffragette movement. She was also one of the town's most vociferous anti-war campaigners, and a supporter of Sylvia Pankhurst's breakaway suffrage movement. Some years after Alice's death, Sylvia Pankhurst would write that she was a 'hardworking, kindly widow . . . the kind of zealous energetic voluntary worker who is the backbone of any movement'.

Alice was certainly zealous in her beliefs. And her daughter Hettie, who was working as a teacher in Ilkeston, was later described as being of 'advanced revolutionary tendencies'. Hettie had served for a time as the local secretary of the NCF, a role she later ceded to a local councillor, Reuben Farrow.

Farrow was a pacifist and a Socialist but, unlike the Wheeldons, his pacifism was rooted in religious, rather than political, beliefs. A devout Christian, Farrow was deeply involved with the Pleasant Sunday Afternoons movement, which hoped to draw working-class adults into churches and church-halls for hymn singing and religious instruction in a less formal, less intimidating setting than a regular service. His less aggressive, more devout stance against the war was not to the taste of the more militant Wheeldons. Hettie in particular, an atheist, seemed to hate all things Christian, noting in a letter: 'I'm not a Christian, therefore not a hypocrite.' She was also passionate in her extreme Socialism, in one letter to an NCF colleague hailing the 'convulsive death rattle of Capitalism'.

After she had given up her role in the NCF, Hettie was notably dismissive of its work, or at least its effects. In a letter to Winnie of 14 January 1917, she wrote: 'The NCF has failed and is dying a natural death.' Money, which was provided by the NCF to the wives and families of those COs on the run or in jail, was in short supply and there were a great many dependants struggling to make ends meet. However, letters between Hettie and her sister Winnie reveal that Hettie continued to work closely with trades union man Arthur McManus in securing the escape of many COs to the safety of the United States. In a letter to Winnie written on

14 January 1917 Hettie was careful not to give away specifics: 'Am making inquiries about the herring pond but its so difficult as Mc's letters are all opened and a personal interview is the only thing.' The herring pond was a common term for the Atlantic Ocean. If they were intercepting Arthur McManus's correspondence, the authorities seemed not to realise that Hettie and her mother had assisted in hiding the Socialist and conscientious objector John S. Clarke at Turner's farm at Arleston, just outside Derby. The Wheeldons' London Road home, Alice's shop on Pear Tree Road, and a house a few hundred yards from there, noted in the 1915–16 directory as the home of Miss Harriett Ann Wheeldon at 7 Byron Street, were all probably also used as refuges for COs.

Young Winnie, too, was an ardent Socialist. Both she and Hettie had attended the Stockwell British and Foreign School Society's Training College in Lambeth and were considered 'very clever girls'. While studying there, Winnie spent many weekends in the company of Derby's MP J.H. (Jimmy) Thomas. A staunch trades unionist and railwayman, Thomas would eventually become general secretary of the National Union of Railwaymen. He had been elected to Parliament on a platform of higher taxation of the rich and the abolition of the House of Lords. He spoke publicly against military conscription, but supported the war effort. Winnie shared his hatred of conscription, calling it in a letter to her family in Derby 'industrial conscription (alias National Service)'.

Winnie was initially reported to have been a confirmed atheist, but for a time became very devoutly Christian, regularly attending the church of St John the Divine in Kennington Road, Lambeth, a 'ritualistic' Anglican church. The other Wheeldons did not entirely eschew spiritual matters either. Alice and her son William are believed to have dabbled in spiritualism, and both Hettie and Winnie taught Scripture in schools. In the summer of 1914 fellow students recalled Winnie arguing with her college professor about the use of 'violence and outrage' in the suffrage movement.

Sometime during her studies Winnie met a young chemist named Alfred Mason. He had qualified in London and had been working at Guy's Hospital's Analytical Department. On 29 May 1915 the 21-year-old Winnie Wheeldon, now using the additional middle name 'Mary' which did not appear on her birth certificate, married Alfred George Mason, one year her senior, at Southampton Register Office. Winnie had been living at 100 Willfield Way, Golders Green, while 'Alph', as Winnie often preferred to spell his name, had found a home and employment back in his home town of Southampton.

Alf Mason's own family could best be described as colourful. He was the son of Rosetta and George Miles Mason. His father has been variously described as an astronomer and an optician, although on Alf's marriage certificate he is listed as an artist, and on the census of 1901 he is recorded as a maker of lantern slides. There were also suggestions of family involvement in the occult. Recent research by Philip Heselton into the witchcraft revival popularised by Gerald Gardner in the 1950s identified Alf's siblings, Ernie, Susie and Rosetta, as members of the so-called 'New Forest Coven' into which Gardner claimed to have been initiated in the 1930s. There is some controversy as to whether the coven really existed in the form Gardner described, or whether he exaggerated its activities for effect, but contemporaries recalled that Ernie at least claimed to have been self-aware from the moment of his birth and he was even described by one acquaintance as a 'genuine witch'. Rosetta dabbled in Anthroposophy, a 'spiritual science' founded by Croatian-born Rudolf Steiner, while Susie had an interest in Theosophy, a religious philosophy which takes elements from many religions, both Western and Eastern, including those of reincarnation and the special significance of the number seven. The family were also said to be involved in Co-Freemasonry, a dissident form of Freemasonry to which both men and women were admitted. Quite how far these esoteric interests had progressed by the time Alf encountered the rebellious Winnie is unknown. What is clear is that the

Masons were broad-minded, liberal and open to and interested in all manner of spiritual beliefs both ancient and new.

Alf himself had begun an apprenticeship, aged 16, with Mr Martin, a chemist of 118 High Street, Southampton. At the age of 20 he had moved to London and Guy's Hospital. He returned to work in Southampton for Mr Martin, and in June 1916 had taken work with Mr Phillip Eley of Shirley Road, Southampton, and was also working as a lecturer at Hartley University.

In contrast to her sisters, observers noted, Nellie appeared 'to be of a more ordinary and milder type [of Socialist]'. Although in later years she would appear to have become more politically active, she confined herself to working at her mother's shop, and her interests in militancy at this stage were still developing through the interests of her family and her exposure to radicals like McManus and Paul, who visited her mother and sister.

Alice's son William was also a confirmed Socialist and pacifist. On 31 August 1916 he appeared before Derby Borough Police Court charged with wilfully obstructing police officers in the execution of their duty. The court heard how, a week earlier, five COs were being transferred from the County Gaol in Vernon Street to Derby Midland station. As the men were being got ready just after noon, around a hundred demonstrators had gathered in the large space in front of the prison. Most were hostile towards the COs, but several were the men's supporters and sympathisers. The prison officers called for police assistance. When the men and their military and civilian police escort emerged from the prison, the sympathisers had surged forward hoping to shake hands with the COs. There was no attempt to rescue them but the escort became worried that the men – who were dressed in civilian garb and not handcuffed – would nevertheless be swallowed up into the crowd. In Friar Gate, a couple of hundred yards from the prison gates, Will Wheeldon had been prominent in trying to impede the police officers, walking slowly in front of them and generally getting in their way. When asked to move, he had shouted: 'Is this a public highway? Are you allowed to walk upon it? I'm not under military discipline and you aren't going to push me about like this. We have plenty of money behind us and the law is always on the side of money.' The newspaper report of the trial deleted an expletive that Will had apparently uttered immediately before the word 'money'.

By the time the prisoners, their escort and the crowd of followers had reached Victoria Street in the town centre, the whole affair had descended into chaos and it was decided to put the prisoners on a tram-car for the rest of their journey down London Road towards the railway station.

When he gave evidence, Will told the court that he was at the Friar Gate end of Vernon Street when the prison gates had been opened. On four or five previous occasions he had been present when COs had been similarly moved, and on those occasions friends and relatives had been allowed to converse with them freely. On this occasion he had seen three friends among the prisoners and wanted to talk to them. But as he was approaching one man, a policeman had grabbed Will by the shoulders and thrown him to one side with the words: 'Get out of it, you dirty coward.' The officer, he said, 'had lost his head and was shaking like a leaf'.

The court was not sympathetic. Will Wheeldon was found guilty and offered a choice: a fine of 50s or one month's imprisonment. He chose gaol. Upon his release, anticipating that he would soon be forced either to join up or be returned to prison, he absconded. Letters between the Wheeldons in Derby and the Masons in Southampton indicate that Will Wheeldon was in hiding near Winnie and Alf in Southampton. Although the recipient's name is not mentioned, one letter from Winnie to her mother mentions gifts and home comforts that have clearly been sent down from Derby: 'Don't send any more socks. He's more than he wants now and so Alph has collared two pairs.' She also noted: 'They [presumably Will and another CO] wuz over here last night and we had a whist drive. Alph won and I had booby.'

Money, too, was being sent down to Southampton. In a letter of late December 1916 Winnie wrote: 'Well dunna send any more money over – Will's got a quid on him for any emergency and odd money too. He's having to buy no tobacco and nowt else so he doesn't need any you see. With the other you sent I paid his grub and lodging bill and Alph and I made up a big parcel of groceries and sent over, so he'll get his share orlright.'

On 7 January 1917, in a letter mainly taken up with complaints about the inclement weather, Winnie reported: 'We haven't been over to the farm today as I didna feel up to much.' Perhaps this reveals the type of hiding place her brother was using. There are no other clues as to why the teacher and her chemist husband might be regular visitors to a local farm.

Despite their separation, the Wheeldons tried to maintain normal family life. In a letter to the Masons, Alice writes of a 'humming bird' that she intends to cook and send down to Winnie 'ready for the Birfday on Wed'. The letter is post-marked 26 January 1917, a Friday; the following Wednesday was William Marshall Wheeldon's 25th birthday.

Alice also mentions some money for 'Mrs C'. Presumably this is Mrs Candy, the Masons' neighbour, and possibly landlady, and perhaps a fellow sympathiser. Will was not the only one helped, it seems. Alice discusses money for 'Davis mother'. In an earlier letter, Winnie mentions that 'Alph and Davis Pall want to do summat re concentration etc. Like the bloke in prison in "The Jacket" used to.' Possible imprisonment was clearly on their minds; the book by Jack London tells the story of a convicted murderer serving time in San Quentin prison. His captors torture him using a device known as a jacket, which compresses his body and causes immense pain. The prisoner manages to overcome the discomfort by entering a trance-like state.

For several months Alf's profession had protected him from conscription but the Wheeldons and Masons knew that it was likely he would soon be called up. He too would need to go into hiding, if he were determined to avoid imprisonment. In late December Winnie asked her mother and sister whether anything has been sorted out for her 'darling Alph . . . he's the sort of chap who'd live in a room for weeks with his books and no one need ever know he was there if he were smuggled into a house and lived in his bedroom. Could he live in the shed on the field?'

Some of the Wheeldons' letters reveal a desire for political change; others pass on details of the various uprisings in the north. Hettie wrote to Winnie in January 1917:

> Have you heard of the mutiny at Darlington? 5 officers have been killed . . . wish it would spread. The Clyde engineers are out again and fighting the soldiers at the gates who were put there to keep them in with crow-bars. Oh missis some stuff.

Their main concerns, however, appear to have been for the COs they sought to protect. Hettie wrote to her sister:

> Sutton is still workless, and living on his sister who has three children, and an income of 30s a week besides helping to pay off money [owed] by that brother of Suttons who drowned himself three years ago so she's live isn't she and all the NCF can allow is 3s some weeks 4s others . . . Frank Burton is still waiting to be seized by the clutching hand and Pall has been completely turned down at the Appeals Tribunal.

The spectre of that 'clutching hand', in the form of the police at least, was never far from their door. On 14 January 1917 Hettie wrote to Winnie:

> Hayward was in his shop when Ada Hayward saw Spiby's [a Derby policeman] shadow on the window.

She kept him talking while Art escaped through the back door. We fitted him up in workmen's overalls and dinner basket and he's 'opped it. Mac [presumably Alexander Macdonald] is terrified. Sticks in all day and only emerges at night. They can no longer employ him. Mac has written for that address.

A week or so later Alice wrote to 'Winn and Alf' about their CO friends: 'Haywood [*sic*: presumably Ada Hayward's husband] and Moss is in the Guard Room at N.B. [probably Normanton Barracks]. Sutcliffe out of work time up today. Sutton expecting arrest any time. Mac out of work lying low only night calls.'

Hettie also indicated her distaste for those who had chosen to accept the call to arms. An old acquaintance, Edwin Baker, 'called yesterday yarning American & doggerel French . . . such as parlez vous pickaxe pomme de terre comme la Gee Ja ete ad nauseum . . . He's been in the Sommey [presumably the Somme] and wears his black and green patch on his arm to announce the fact.' But it was not just friends who had joined up. Their brother-in-law John Vernon, married to their half-sister Lily, was 'in Notts Hospital – shellshock. Lily won't go to see him. Doesn't want to see him again alive or dead.' It remained unclear whether Lily's attitude was due to an objection to the war, an emotional reaction to his condition, or simply a marriage already in terminal decline.

In one letter, signed only '10', an imprisoned CO who had once worked closely with Hettie in the NCF wrote to her via his mother. The letter appears to have been smuggled out of a detention centre. He mentions several of his fellow inmates, many of whom are clearly familiar to the Wheeldons; men like 'long lost Barry' and George Smith. Merry of Nottingham and Christopher Thorpe of Heanor 'have done two months at Wormwood and have refused the HO work. Put them on the Roll of Obstructers. Neither belongs to the NCF but I think I can induce Thorpe to join. He doesn't claim to be religious, so that is a good sign.' He also notes, undoubtedly with a great deal of irony: 'No one likes to leave here, it is so "cushy";' and he quotes a poem popular with the inmates:

There's everything for nothing
And you never spend a cent
And the landlord, ha, ha, ha, ha
He never calls for rent.

Conditions, however, were far from cushy and the letter tells how the guards had forcibly cut the writer's hair, even though he had struggled so much they had needed to force him to the floor on his knees before the task could be completed. Poignantly, he asks: 'How are women taking the "calling to slaughter" of their 18-year-old boys? Will they never protest? Or will they keep on saying: "What has to be will be"?'

Because of the nature of their activities, the Wheeldons were only too aware of the need for secrecy and discretion. They were careful to avoid specific details and not to give away locations of safe houses. They developed codes known only to themselves and urged caution: 'Keep quiet that's the thing. They haven't a notion of anybody's whereabouts,' wrote Hettie to her younger sister. She had advice for her brother-in-law too: 'Tell Alf as soon as the push becomes hot to make a bee-line for here and then things can be considered. I've several suggestions but haven't the time to put them in code now and of course I won't write them.' A letter from 'Mam' to Winnie noted: 'I don't think the last letter in parcel was opened . . . was it sewed up with string all right, if so it had not been tampered with.'

For all her militancy, Alice was known among her friends for her warm and generous nature. She had a particular openness among those whom she regarded as allies. Winnie, it seems, was concerned that this openness might cause her mother to trust her perceived allies with more information than was necessary, or safe. In one letter she told Alice that, for security's sake, they should change the key word in their code:

> There are too many in the secret now, and it may leak out. A secret known to more than two is not much good anytime, and more so now. Anyhow, it will do the nosey parkers who read private letters a bit of good to puzzle their putrid pulp over a new one . . . trust absolutely nobody . . . The only ones to trust are ourselves. I don't want you to involve yourself in any useless risk for anything. I should not let Mac or Paul or Robbs or any of them [know] about anything which they don't already know . . . inform people about what they've found for themselves.

But there was little that Winnie could do to caution Alice against helping those in need of her contacts. For any desperate CO, Alice Wheeldon always had an open door and a warm and sympathetic heart. Despite her obvious intellect, this generosity of spirit, combined with a steely determination to help, an enthusiasm for her chosen cause that bordered on the obsessive, and a radical willingness to act, left Alice vulnerable to two opportunistic individuals who were about to make her acquaintance.

On 27 December 1916 a roughly dressed young man arrived at Alice's door. He told her that his name was Alex Gordon and that he was a CO. Someone at Derby's Clarion Club in the Wardwick had sent him to her. Such a recommendation was not unusual and Alice gave him two addresses where he might safely spend the night. At one, the home of Miss Marsden at 34 Hartington Street, he got no reply; at the second, that of Mrs Lydia Robinson of Wye Street in the suburb of Alvaston, he received a warm reception. Two days later Gordon returned to the Wheeldons' and introduced a friend of his, Herbert Norton, or 'Comrade Bert' as Gordon called him. He, too, was apparently a CO. Both professed to know Arthur McManus from

Liverpool, and it did appear that Gordon, at least, had made prior contact with him. Later, he would claim that Norton 'told her I had been on the run since September as a moral objector'.

But neither Gordon nor Norton was who he purported to be. Both were agents in the employ of the Ministry of Munitions. More specifically they were working for the Parliamentary Military Section 2 (PMS2), sent out to gather intelligence on potential industrial unrest that might hinder the war effort. Norton, whose real name was Herbert Booth, was in fact Gordon's superior rather than his friend. And rather than being Alice's allies, both Booth and Gordon were busy filing reports on her activities, reports so alarming that a legal case was beginning to form against the family, who had been right to exercise caution in their correspondence; for weeks every letter that had passed between them had been intercepted, read and copied by Booth's and Gordon's bosses.

Within days the Wheeldons of Derby found themselves the subject of extraordinary accusations of treasonous plotting and intent to murder.

Chapter 6

Centre of Interest

On the morning of Wednesday, 31 January 1917 the people of Derby awoke to find that their unassuming town had, overnight, become a centre of interest and intrigue throughout the Western world. National daily newspapers had been the first to break the news: several members of a Derby family had been arrested and charged with plotting to murder the British Prime Minister and one of his ministers.

By the time the first edition of the *Derby Daily Telegraph*, carrying the headline SENSATIONAL CONSPIRACY CHARGE IN DERBY, DERBY PEOPLE CHARGED, reached the town's parlours, offices and factories around lunchtime, there could have been few Derbeians unaware of the extraordinary story that was unfolding on their doorsteps. The Wheeldon family of Pear Tree Road, already known for their radicalism and support of conscientious objectors, stood accused of a terrible crime against the country. It was well known that there was a network of safe havens for COs in the town, and that members of the Wheeldon family attended CO hearings, cheering the prisoners as they were taken to prison. It took no effort at all to link the two elements. And little more to link the Wheeldons with the charges on which they were being held.

By the end of that day news of the remarkable charges had spread across the Empire and beyond. The *Lowell Sun* – the local paper of a town in Massachusetts with long-standing Derby connections – reported in great detail the 'Plot to Murder British Leaders'. By the following day the sensational news had reached the western half of the North American continent; in Canada the *Manitoba Press* also dwelt enthusiastically on the 'three Suffragettes and a conscientious objector to military service' who had been arrested. The newspaper assured its readers that 'the conservative British law, circumscribing matters which the newspapers may print in advance of court proceedings, insures against any efforts in the press to arouse feeling against them'. Nevertheless, the majority of British people already displayed plenty of animosity towards both Suffragists and so-called conchies; now the nation's newspapers, usually full of anti-German propaganda, had a new target at which to aim.

Back in Derby, each revelation, each astonishing detail, was devoured by a public previously focused entirely on the progress of the war, a public more used to reading officially sanctioned, sometimes relentlessly cheerful, news from the battle front. That very morning the newspapers had concentrated on the 'complete failure' of the latest German attack on the Belgian Front. Now, however, details of the arrest warrants were of primary interest:

> To each and all of the Constables of the said County Borough.
>
> Information on oath has been laid this day by Edward Parker, of New Scotland Yard, London, Inspector of Police, on behalf of the Director of Public Prosecutions, that ALICE WHEELDON and HETTIE WHEELDON of 12 Pear Tree Road, Derby, and WINNIE MASON and ALFRED GEORGE MASON, of 172 Millbrook Road, Southampton, hereinafter called the defendants, on divers days

between the 26th day of December 1916 and the date
of laying this information, at the County Borough
aforesaid, did amongst themselves unlawfully and
wickedly conspire, confederate and agree together
one the Right Honourable David Lloyd George, and
one the Right Honourable Arthur Henderson wilfully
and of their malice aforethought to kill and murder,
contrary to the Offences against the Person Act, 1861,
section 4, and against the peace etc.

YOU ARE THEREFORE HEREBY COMMANDED to bring the
defendants before the Court of Summary Jurisdiction.

Up to now, the British people had known the identity of their
enemy – a familiar, almost cartoon-like, foe that was regarded
both as peculiar and wicked in the extreme. The *Derby Daily
Telegraph* had, that very morning, declared that to the
German people 'there is nothing revolting in the wholesale
murder that their rulers contemplate with such fiendish glee
in search of world domination'. The newspaper had written of
the 'Unspeakable Turk' who, Reuter's News Agency had
reported, was attempting to 'exterminate Arabs' in Armenia
and Lebanon. But now people were faced with a new adversary, and one that had sought to strike at the very soul of the
country, from its own back streets – an enemy within. The
Wheeldons were about to find the enthusiastic reporting style
of the British press pointed firmly in their direction.

There was no escaping the war. Among the advertisements
for Artificial Teeth and Theaker's Salmon Paste were those
placed by local tailor E.H. Simpson of St James's Street, who
promoted 'Officer's Kit at short notice – style and fit guaran-
teed, correct in every detail'. Photographer Pollard Graham, of
the Rodney Yard, recommended 'The Bijou Portrait' which
was 'designed specially for carrying in a pocket. Most suitable
for soldiers and sailors.' And alongside them were reports of
hospitals being filled with wounded soldiers, and details of
local men who had lost their lives. Coinciding with the

Wheeldon sensation were several fatalities with local connections, among them 24-year-old Lieutenant Charles Cadman of the Royal Engineers, a former pupil of the town's ancient Derby School, who had been awarded the Military Cross before he was killed in France.

Another of the town's young men reported dead was Tom Bradley, an engine-room artificer 3rd class on HM Submarine *K13*. He was the son of Tom and Katie Bradley, who lived in Sale Street, near Alice's shop. He was killed, along with thirty-one others, when their submarine sank after letting in water as it practised diving in a Scottish loch.

With so many people preoccupied with the fighting of the war, with shortages and hardship, with fear for loved ones serving abroad, with compassion for the wounded and sick, and with grief for the sons, fathers, brothers and sweethearts whose lives had been lost, it is little wonder that the townsfolk of Derby were so bewildered by the astonishing allegations against the Wheeldons. That such a threat – to a man described by the Pennsylvanian *Clearfield Progress* as 'England's Man of the Hour' – could come from within their own community was an even greater shock.

The focus of the police investigation had been on Alice Wheeldon's shop in Pear Tree Road, but the spotlight of public attention was on the town's nineteenth-century Guildhall in the Market Place. The building served both as Derby's town council headquarters and its courtroom, and it was in the dark wood-panelled council chamber itself, beneath the solemn gaze of many former mayors whose portraits hung high on the walls, that legal proceedings got under way at 11am.

Although the police court proceedings at this stage were little more than a formality, this did little to calm the mood of the dozens of onlookers who had gathered in the Market Place to witness the spectacle; the *Derby Daily Telegraph* reported 'an unusual air of animation in the neighbourhood'. As the defendants were brought in, silence fell over the court. Mr

W.B. Whiston, the magistrates' clerk, read out the charges as laid by Inspector Edward Parker of Scotland Yard. Mr S. Pearce, acting on behalf of the Director of Public Prosecutions, noted that the hearing was simply a matter of remanding the prisoners in custody for a few days, and did little to outline the precise nature of the case. However, details of the timing and manner of the four arrests were put before the court.

Alice Wheeldon had been the first arrest target. When Inspector William Higham and PC Spiby (incorrectly referred to as Spilsby in some newspapers) of Derby Borough Police, accompanied by Detective Sergeant Halley of Scotland Yard, arrived at 12 Pear Tree Road, Alice was nowhere to be seen. Spiby, who had been the first to enter the premises, did find the unfortunate Alexander Mann Macdonald, who had been absent without leave from the Sherwood Foresters since December 1916. Inevitably Macdonald was arrested and charged.

Higham had then entered the premises and encountered Alfred Mason. After listening to the details of the warrant for his arrest, Mason had said simply: 'Not Guilty.' Among the papers taken from Mason's person were his registration card, a certificate from the Pharmacists' Society, a passport application, and details of the schedule of steamers bound for the United States. On the way to the nearby Bloomfield Street police station, Mason had said little, except to state that he had left Southampton, by bicycle, on Saturday morning and arrived in Derby the same night.

At 12.45pm the officers returned to 12 Pear Tree Road and shortly thereafter Alice Wheeldon was arrested. When the accusation was put to her, she said simply: 'I have nothing to say about it.' She was also taken to the police station in Bloomfield Street and thereafter to the lock-up next to the Guildhall. Eliza Walden, matron of the lock-up, would later testify that she had searched Alice and found only some insurance papers.

The officers had then travelled to Ilkeston where they

arrested Hettie Wheeldon at work at about 2.15pm. The school's headmaster, Mr A. Beacroft, had summoned her from her class and pupils watched from their classroom window as two men wearing bowler hats guided Hettie into a horse-drawn carriage. Again, a short denial was given, but Alice's daughter immediately made clear her political stance: 'I am the organiser of the CO in Derby. I found it too much for me. I have handed it over to Mr Farrow.' Of the alleged plot, she said only: 'I know the people you mean [it would have been more remarkable had she not], but I know nothing about the murder charge.' Hettie Wheeldon was also taken to the lock-up where Eliza Walden found a letter and what appeared to be a crib to their secret code, as well as copies of *The Tribune* and *The Socialist*.

On the south coast, meanwhile, Detective-Inspector John McCormac of Southampton Borough Police, accompanied by Inspector Parker of Scotland Yard's CID and assisted by Inspector Fred Everest, had arrested Winnie Mason at Foundry Lane Council School. 'What is it all about? I don't understand it!' she protested before coming close to a confession – at least of her situation, if not her guilt: 'I know how much I am in it.' She also confirmed her husband's story about him cycling to Derby, en route to Liverpool, where he intended to seek work. Parker and his sergeant, Percival Hallett, searched their home and the prisoner was then transferred to Derby.

With so few details available, the *Derby Daily Telegraph* made much of the Wheeldons' existing notoriety following Will Wheeldon's activities. William Marshall Wheeldon, the paper told its readers, 'figured very prominently last year in the ranks of the conscientious objectors to military service'. By now, the paper noted, with no little relish, his whereabouts were unknown, having become an 'absentee from military service'. It has to be noted that it was Alice Wheeldon who brought up the subject of her CO son at the hearing. She was in no doubt why she had been singled out in this way:

> I think it is such a trumped-up charge to punish me
> for my lad being a conscientious objector . . . you
> punished him through me while you had him in
> prison . . . you brought up an unfounded charge that
> he went to prison for and now he has gone out of the
> way you think you will punish him through me and
> you will do it.

The Wheeldon women's support for 'suffragist propaganda'
was also noted in the local newspaper, although (and this is
perhaps evidence of the town's traditionally liberal and
Socialist nature) the writer did concede that such a belief 'is,
of course, no more against them than it would be against
millions of other women possessed of equal intelligence and
education'.

Other than their brief protestations of innocence, the
Wheeldons confined their comments to complaints about the
conditions in which they had been held overnight. Because
the county prison in Vernon Street was now in the hands
of the military authorities, they had been taken to the town's
primitive lock-up, which stood beside both the police station
and Guildhall. 'My feet have not been warm since I went there.
The disgraceful state of the place and its coldness are a
disgrace to civilisation,' complained Alice. Although the lock-
up was convenient for the Guildhall, the accused were
reassured that, since the various legal proceedings were likely
to take some weeks, they would now be taken to the relatively
more comfortable Birmingham prison.

Over the next few days readers of the *Derby Daily Telegraph*
were presented with an enormous amount of background
information on the defendants, from their political leanings to
their employment history. Further details of the alleged crimes
were revealed at the magisterial hearing that began on
Saturday, 3 February, by which time the *Derby Daily
Telegraph* was calling it 'The Great Conspiracy Charge'.

Again the proceedings were held in the council chamber

amid an 'atmosphere of mystery'. Hundreds of people queued outside, hoping to observe at first hand the extraordinary proceedings within. The magistrates who would hear the proceedings were, in their own right, some of Derby's most influential men. Henry Bonas, a tape manufacturer who owned one of the town's biggest mills, lived in a large house at 110 Uttoxeter New Road and was the current mayor. The previous mayor, Alderman Albert Green, another textile manufacturer, also served on the town's conscientious objector tribunal. Sir Thomas Roe now served as the town's MP, having himself been a councillor for more than fifty years and mayor three times, most recently in 1910. William Gilbert Haslam was a town councillor of some standing; he was a member of an influential family of founders and resided at the splendid Breadsall Priory, just outside the town. The other magistrates, William Eaton, Robert Hudson, William Cooper and Thomas Wigley, were also highly respected men.

While the Wheeldons and Masons were represented by Mr R.S. Clifford, a relatively humble Derby solicitor who had offices in Full Street, the DPP brought out the big guns and, as if to reinforce the severity of the charges, appointed as prosecutor the Attorney-General himself, Sir Frederick Smith, who had been instrumental in the bringing of charges in the first place. Smith, the MP for Liverpool Walton, had previously been in charge of the government's Press Bureau, which was responsible for newspaper censorship. In 1915 he had been appointed Solicitor-General and not long afterwards had replaced Sir Edward Carson as Attorney-General. He had a number of friends in high places and, on the night Asquith had resigned as Prime Minister in 1916, had been hosting a dinner party at which David Lloyd George, Max Aitken and Winston Churchill had been his guests. In the same year Smith had secured the conviction and execution of the Irish nationalist Sir Roger Casement, who had been charged with treason after attempting to obtain German support for the Irish cause.

Smith was a renowned orator of great passion and on this particular morning in Derby was quick to outline the devious nature of the defendants. As the *Washington Post* reported, Smith 'referred to the prisoners as desperate, dangerous people, bitterly hostile to the country'. They were, he declared, 'shelterers of fugitives from the army who were doing their best to injure Great Britain in her present crisis'. There were many watching who would have readily imposed long custodial sentences on such people, murder plot or not.

That the prosecution would immediately attempt to cast a shadow on the characters of the defendants was unremarkable and, quite probably, the oldest legal trick in the book. What did cause a stir was Smith's sudden announcement that secret undercover operatives had gathered much of the evidence that he would put before the court: 'The Sensational Conspiracy Charge – the Attorney-General's Startling Revelation,' reported the *Derby Daily Telegraph*. According to the newspaper, Smith had assured the astonished court that 'in days like these it was evident that those responsible for the government and safety of this country must employ secret agents'. Smith explained that such an agent, working under the name Alex Gordon, had been sent to Derby towards the end of December. If onlookers had expected to hear the agent's testimony, they were quickly disappointed. 'I take the responsibility for deciding . . . for reasons which seem to me good, not to call this witness before the court,' Smith announced. Another agent, one Herbert Booth, did appear and there would be plenty of witness statements for the court to consider as well as a large number of letters submitted, all of which had either been intercepted by the authorities while in transit, or discovered at the defendants' homes following their arrests.

As if all the excitement of secret government agents was not enough, Smith's revelation of the intended murder weapon – the exotic poison curare – was more than enough to keep the pages of the *Derby Daily Telegraph* filled with feature articles over the weekend. The paper presented a great deal of background information under the title: 'The Poison in the Case – the Mysteries of Curare – Used by Indians for Barbing Arrows.' There were features, too, on other elements of the case made public by the Attorney-General.

A link was made between the case and the 'Burning of Breadsall Church', with Booth's claims that both Nellie and Alice had boasted of their responsibility for the fire. Of course, the court had only the word of a government agent to go on, with no independent witness, and it was unclear, even if it were true that Nellie and Alice had made those statements, whether they were claiming personal responsibility, or doing so on behalf of the Suffragist movement. Nevertheless, it served to all but confirm the long-held belief locally that the Suffragettes had been responsible for the fire, and it was the nearest the Derby public had come to hearing an admission of guilt. Flame-damaged churches aside, Emmeline Pankhurst must have been made incandescent by this testimony. It was hardly surprising then, but to no small excitement, that 'Mrs Pankhurst, the leader of the Suffragette movement, had arrived in the town with the intention of being present during the proceedings and, if permitted, of making a statement'.

As it turned out, Emmeline Pankhurst was, understandably, determined to draw a very clear and very broad line between herself and her movement and the Wheeldons and their alleged crimes. It would do her cause no good at all to be associated with allegations of a plot to murder the Prime Minister. It later transpired that Mrs Pankhurst had been unable to make her statement to the court because the counsel for the defence had successfully argued that such a statement might 'impugn the veracity of the defence' and would thus prejudice the case against his clients. Later correspondence revealed that the Suffragette had merely wanted to put on record that the WSPU had formulated no plans to kill anyone. However, the prosecution clearly thought such a statement might also prejudice its own case, and declared it had no intention of calling her as a witness. She would have to wait to plead her organisation's innocence.

If the Wheeldons had spent a more comfortable two nights in Birmingham, the disadvantages of being transported over a greater distance soon became clear. The daily trip through Derby's main railway station became ever more perilous. Crowds of onlookers gathered to see the accused as they arrived, and many were not content with simply gaping. Several 'displayed some hostility towards them'. Reports suggested that there was 'much booing and pushing' and this eventually necessitated 'police protection'. Hettie noted that, on one occasion, their return journey was observed by Sir Archibald Bodkin, one of the prosecutors.

Despite the number of witnesses, many of whom were brought in from Southampton, the hearing was completed by Tuesday, 6 February and the defendants were committed for trial. Formal assizes before a Grand Jury were set for the following day. By 1917 the role of a Grand Jury was merely to ratify a defendant's committal for trial and it rarely put up any opposition to the process. Even Mr Justice Rowlatt, presiding over the court that day, noted: 'It may be right to abolish the Grand Jury system altogether.' However, if the Wheeldons were expecting the judge's address to be a mere formality, they were to be disappointed. Although it had already been informally agreed that the full trial should take place in London rather than in Derby, Rowlatt took it upon himself to outline the details once more, and to express his personal opinion of the nature of those accused: 'One could not help expressing wonder that women such as these were revealed by their correspondence to be, should be in a position to teach the young.'

And, just in case any member of the Grand Jury was in any doubt, Rowlatt outlined the crimes of conspiracy and murder and reinforced the severity of such crimes:

Of course, it is a most serious crime to conspire to murder at any time. To conspire to murder a Minister of the Crown, for a supposed political object, is at any time a most sinister thing. At the present moment to conspire to murder, and to murder by poison, the first Minister of the Crown and one of his associates seems to pass beyond the description that I have applied to the crime in general and become a felon blow attempted against the safety of our country.

Mr H. Maddocks, representing the Crown, might well have taken pride in making such a speech himself.

Just before 3pm the Grand Jury arrived at its inevitable decision to send the accused for trial. Alice and Hettie Wheeldon and Alfred and Winnie Mason were brought from the cells and stood in the dock as their solicitor spoke to them through the rails to advise them of their situation. They spoke only to accept the request that the trial be transferred to London.

The first act of a drama that had begun in a small provincial courtroom was over; the second would be continued on the London judicial stage.

Chapter 7

An Infamous Concoction

The relocation of the criminal trial of the Wheeldons and the Masons to London, and to the most famous court in England, the Old Bailey, proved somewhat controversial. Although the accused had formally accepted it, there were suspicions, among their friends and allies at least, that the change of venue took full advantage of the recent Zeppelin attacks on the capital. It made for a prospective jury that was likely to be both frightened of the enemy and sound in their determination to win the war.

Yet it was difficult to argue against the decision. The trial was as high profile as any in recent years. An alleged plot against the Prime Minister was obviously of national importance. The prosecution had pointed out that it would be difficult to find jurymen in Derby who would not be biased in their opinion of the Wheeldons; details of their personalities, beliefs and habits, as well as the case against them, had been outlined in such detail that there could be few in the town who were not familiar with almost every aspect of it. If the family had endured a bad reputation before their arrests, Attorney-General Sir Frederick Smith had ensured that, by the end of the hearings, their reputation was in tatters.

On the morning of Tuesday, 6 March 1917, less than five weeks after their arrests, Alice and Hettie Wheeldon and Alfred and Winnie Mason took their places in the dock of Court no. 2 of the Central Criminal Court. Squashed into the narrow street after which it was named, the Old Bailey had been built only ten years earlier, on the site of the notorious Newgate prison.

Yet as prestigious and modern a legal venue as the Old Bailey then was, there were complaints from one correspondent for the *Derby Mercury* that no. 2 Court was a 'little court, rather pokey', and that 'Derby Guildhall makes a much better stage, providing ten times the accommodation for the interested public'. And, indeed, the interested public numbered many. The environs of the court were 'besieged by holders of tickets. A number of ladies, several having the distinction of titles, presented themselves and, after their permits had been scrutinised, they were admitted', reported the *Derby Daily Telegraph*. With enormous press interest, the court was soon filled to capacity. Proceedings got under way at 10am, with the arrival of the twelve male jurors; in 1917, of course, women were not permitted to sit on a jury.

The Wheeldons now had a new attorney. While on remand Hettie had written to her brother William, who had since been captured and interned, about the family's concerns over their Derby lawyer: 'What Clifford is doing I don't know. We've neither heard from nor seen him yet. Whether he is weaving a new web to catch us in I don't know . . . it has been decided from the beginning that we are not to be allowed to make a defence.'

Papers in the possession of Fay Kidger, the granddaughter of Lydia Robinson, the NCF supporter who had first taken Gordon in, extracts from which were published in the *Derby Evening Telegraph* in 1983, suggest that the Derby solicitors ceased to act for the family one week before the trial, their bill of almost £67 not having been paid. In a letter to Mrs Robinson, dated 24 February, Hettie notes that a new lawyer was about to be appointed, and that Miss Marsden of the NCF was assisting the family in their choice of attorney.

Now only one man, and his assistant solicitor, stood between the defendants and the might of the English legal system: Saiyid Haidan Riza, who was, it seemed, a man of some mystery to the members of the press. A barrister of 4 Essex Court, just off the Strand, he was described variously as a 'dark-skinned Hindu', a 'Mohammedin', a 'Persian', and of 'Indian extraction'. Precise details, it seems, were unimportant; the goal was to point out the defence counsel's foreign appearance, nationality and religion. In fact, in May 1914 Riza, then listed as a 30-year-old law student (he might have been required to requalify for English law) had married Ella Mary Higgins, a Hastings girl, at Islington Register Office. On 19 January 1917, just days before the Wheeldons and the Masons were arrested, Ella Riza had given birth to a son, Saiyid Anthony Peter Imam Riza, at 132 Earls Court Road.

It has been largely assumed that Riza accepted the case when no other was offered to him because of his background, although at least one North American newspaper described him as 'the noted criminal lawyer'. The *Derby Mercury*, meanwhile, reported that he had some high-profile legal experience, having conducted an appeal by anti-government Irish nationalist MP Laurence Ginnell. It is certainly true that the Wheeldons were not blessed with a queue of willing top-notch advocates ready to take up their case. However, evidence in the files held by the Home Office notes that a man, later tentatively identified as Riza, was observed watching the Derby hearings with great interest. There is a suggestion that he may have been responsible in part for setting up a fund to pay for the defence, and Hettie's letter suggests that he was well known to the Socialist movement. The Home Office report, filed on 12 February 1917 by a senior investigator, noted: 'He has said, I am told, that a good KC will easily smash the case for the prosecution.'

Before he could even begin his work in court, however, Riza

was battling prejudices of his own. As a foreigner, and a non-white one at that, he had to endure editorial comments that veered from patronising to outright mockery at his accent, his appearance and his mannerisms. The *Derby Mercury*, which pronounced him to have 'Persian royal blood in his veins', noted: 'He is rather a little man, approaching middle age [he was 32 or 33], wears a pair of gold-rimmed spectacles of the type Mr Pickwick's pictures have made familiar.' The news-paper then went on to compare him to an offensively stereotypical and patronising fictional creation of *Punch* writer F. Anstey, 'Baboo Hurry Bungsho Jabberjee, BA'. The *Mercury* did provide some further biographical information. Riza, it claimed, had been offered the Persian throne by the 'Revolutionists'.

The large prosecution legal team, meanwhile, was formid-able and already commanded immense respect from the press. At its head, once more, was Attorney-General Sir Frederick Smith. His deputy was Sir Archibald Bodkin, the man who had successfully prosecuted George Joseph Smith, the 'Brides in the Bath' murderer, two years earlier.

Presiding over the whole affair was Mr Justice Low, the former Liberal MP for Norwich. Sir Frederick Low had been knighted in 1909. A few years earlier he had been a regular on the Midland circuit, in particular at the Derby Assizes. A short 60-year-old with 'a sharp, intellectual face', he was, according to the *Derby Mercury*, 'one of our ablest judges'.

Sir Frederick Smith's opening statement had lasted 1 hour and 50 minutes at the Derby hearing, and only 10 minutes less at the Old Bailey. In both he began by citing the terms of the indictment and, according to the *Derby Daily Telegraph*, spoke 'in solemn tones'. The paper reported that Smith went on to suggest that the jury might 'find some psychological clue to the actions of the accused in the hatred which they felt for the two persons mentioned in the indictment'. He pointed out that Alfred Mason was a 'trained and qualified chemist' who had 'made a special study of poisons'. There was also evidence,

Smith noted, to suggest that Alf had a plan in preparation to go on the run in the event of his being called up to the army.

Since the Derby hearings, the general shock at the revelation that secret government agents had been used to gather evidence had subsided, but as Smith began to explain to the Old Bailey jury the importance of employing secret agents 'in certain circumstances', his words were 'listened to with a keen attention by the entire assemblage, legal and lay'. The CO movement was largely underground, Smith told the court, and in order to garner information about it, it was necessary to 'use an affectation of sympathy'. He explained that, given the possibility of encountering sabotage plots by the enemy, such spies worked under 'extremely dangerous' conditions, and because of this it was 'not usual for such persons to discharge their duties in their own names'.

Smith went on to outline how 'a man called Gordon' had gone to Derby where he had met members of the CO movement, including Alice and Hettie Wheeldon, and that subsequently Gordon's immediate superior, Booth, had received a telegram from him informing him of some alarming findings. At this point defence barrister Riza rose to his feet to object, arguing that, if Gordon were not to be called as a witness, then any telegram sent by him could not be admitted to court. Justice Low replied: 'The fact that the telegram was received would surely be within the knowledge of the recipient?' But Riza did not readily submit, arguing that, if Gordon were not to testify, then the veracity of the telegram could not be proved. The judge retorted: 'But there are many ways of proving a telegram without necessarily calling the person who sent it.' And in a somewhat patronising reprimand, he told Riza: 'I think you had better listen to the Attorney's opening, and we will see when the proper time comes.'

At that Riza sat down and Smith took time to reveal what the *Derby Daily Telegraph* described as 'one of the most unedifying features of the case' – Alice's propensity to use 'obscene and disgusting' language, a habit which had spread to her daughters – 'both of whom were engaged as schoolteachers'. Despite their education, Smith noted, the Wheeldon women were 'in the habit of employing, habitually, language which would be disgusting and obscene in the mouth of the lowest class of criminal'.

The Attorney-General then returned to the details of the case against the defendants. He told the jury that the two agents had been involved in discussions with Alice Wheeldon, at her shop on Pear Tree Road, about the possibility of using poison to kill first Lloyd George and then others. They had talked, Smith said, about 'the despatch of a letter to Southampton for poisons' and about the Wheeldons' involvement in the Breadsall Church fire. On 1 January the agents had been party to Alice's concern over the non-arrival of a package containing poisons and witnessed her rant of obscenities against Lloyd George, Arthur Henderson, Asquith and the King. When Booth asked Alice – 'with the object of informing himself as to how far the prisoner intended to proceed in any scheme' – the best way to poison Lloyd George, he had been told, Smith asserted, that Alice had taken part in previous plots to murder the new Prime Minister and another prominent man. While these proposed actions might appear to be the spontaneous manifestations of 'irresponsible rage', Smith intended to prove that 'every detail of the scheme had been thought out'. The Attorney-General then spent some time referring to various apparently incriminating extracts from intercepted correspondence between the family members, in which the women had criticised the war and the nation's leaders.

The prosecution would concentrate its case on a parcel, which was sent by Winnie and Alf from Southampton to their mother in Derby, and which contained various poisons. Smith returned repeatedly to the theme of the 'completely diseased moral condition' of the defendants. He noted that the Masons were prone to using code in certain sections of their letters and that the family as a whole cared little for the lives of those fighting in the trenches, and instead 'reserved their sympathy, their admiration and their succour for the shirkers who avoided the duty of protecting their country'. The defendants, he insisted, were dangerous people who 'held revolutionary views, they plotted to get a distinguished man out of the way, and they took up the task as involving no difficulty whatever'. The jury would, he was sure, 'not fail to do their duty'.

The prosecution then called its first witness: Herbert Booth, the man who had been introduced to the Wheeldons as Comrade Bert, or Herbert Norton. At the Derby hearings Booth had appeared only on the second day, when Sir Frederick Smith was not even in court, and had followed some rather turgid evidence about the arrests and statements from no fewer than five Post Office officials. At the Old Bailey, however, the Attorney-General was more confident in his star witness's persuasiveness and put him at the centre of the case. As he had in Derby, Smith left the examination of his witness to a junior colleague. As Mr Hugo Young took the floor at the Old Bailey, the court fell silent.

Very little was known about Booth. He was born in Southwark, the son of Irish-born journalist Charles Booth, who had also worked as a law writer. Booth, too, had entered the legal world, for many years working as a barrister's clerk. He was married twice, first to Christina Marshall in 1903 at Peckham. She had died shortly after giving birth to a daughter in 1911. In October 1914 Booth married Matilda Firmin, the widowed licensee of the Cock Hotel in the tiny village of Headley in Surrey. Indeed, Booth's involvement with the Wheeldon case and his 'shady dealings' feature prominently on the pub's modern website. Hearsay suggests that Booth had, quite suddenly, disappeared from the family home, his stepdaughter being somewhat surprised when he turned up at the Old Bailey.

Whatever the mysteries of his past, according to the *Derby Mercury* Booth was a 'clean-shaven man about 40 years of age [he was 37], who gave evidence with quiet self-possession'. From his testimony, it is clear that Booth was a man of considerable intelligence, with a dry wit, and a neat understanding of comic timing. He could hold an audience and made an excellent witness.

According to the *Derby Daily Telegraph*, Booth's statement – much of which he read out himself, often referring to a diary in which he had recorded details of his meetings with Alice Wheeldon – 'proved unexpectedly short'. However, it was not without interruption.

Almost as soon as Booth began his account the defence launched its objections, first in regard to a letter of which it had no record. After some argument, the prosecution admitted culpability, having not informed the defence of the letter's inclusion, and yielded. Much of what Booth related only echoed Smith's opening statement about Gordon's contact with the Wheeldons and the supposed poison plot. But it did add some considerable colour and detail.

Although he was a plausible witness, Booth's grasp of detail was still a little shaky. At one point he referred to the 'Independent [rather than International] Workers of the World Movement', and later referred to one of the Ministry of Munitions officials, Colonel Frank A. Labouchere, by the title Major. At Derby, demonstrating a remarkable loss of memory, Booth appeared to have forgotten who 'Win' was, saying: 'I knew who Win was but I cannot remember.' Then: 'I do now remember it was one of Mrs Wheeldon's daughters.' It must have been slightly concerning, especially for the prosecution, that its main witness could not recall one of the accused. Whether these slips might have made the jury doubt the accuracy of the witness before them was unclear because neither error was picked up by the defence.

Booth stated that he had arrived in Derby on 29 December 1916 on the 7pm train. He had been met by Gordon and spent the following day at the station waiting to intercept a package 'about 18ins – box-shaped' which was to be brought there by Hettie Wheeldon. But by early evening neither Hettie nor the package had arrived, so Booth and Gordon had left for Pear

Tree Road. He described how they had all sat around the parlour table as Alice asked Gordon to write a letter to Arthur McManus introducing her son Will, Alexander Mann Macdonald and 'another man' to him. It seems slightly odd that Alice would have asked Gordon to do this; she was already well acquainted with McManus. Having apparently assisted in the 'emigration' of several young COs, she scarcely needed a recommendation. Whether the Ministry of Munitions – or its agents – was aware of quite how close the Wheeldons were to the entire hierarchy of the ILP was never made clear. Booth was certainly aware of the Wheeldons' association with Willie Paul, though. He stated that, when Gordon asked whether he should send Paul's best wishes to McManus, Alice had said: 'I have been with Paul an hour and a half today. When the time comes [to go to ground], he has got a nice soft place near here so that he will be able to see his wife.'

According to Booth, it was only at this point that Alice sought to ask him about himself, having presumably accepted him because he had come with Gordon. Booth supported his story of conscientious objection with what he called 'one or two escapades of getting away from the police'. He had told her that he was at the Great Tongue Yard headquarters of the IWW when it had been raided. When asked about this organisation, Booth had told an amused court: 'They talk sedition, and want the world for themselves.'

Booth said that Alice had shown him photographs of her son, Will:

> As she was showing it to me, she said: 'You know the Breadsall job? We were nearly copped but we bloody well beat them!'
> Her eldest daughter Nellie had added: 'It was a sight when the flames went up.'

Alice, Booth claimed, when asked how the Suffragettes were able to burn down churches, boasted, 'Oh with petrol, we did

it with petrol,' before she 'suddenly changed the expression to
"that's how *they* did it".'

According to Booth, Alice had shown him a bracelet made
from a stuffed snakeskin. The bracelet was brought into court
as Exhibit 17 and Booth told the jury that Alice had told him it
was poisonous and that she wished 'she had a hundred of
them'. Then all at once, stated Booth, 'she turned to Gordon
and said: "You are dead from tonight [pointing at him] you
must keep out of the way".' Gordon answered, 'Right.' Mrs
Wheeldon then said: 'Don't come here until 8.20 Monday.'
Then, he said, Gordon told Alice to send all future messages
through Booth. The conversation had next turned to the NCF
and Booth testified that Alice had criticised Christian Socialist
Reuben Farrow's 'milk and water Jesus Christ manner'.

Booth and Gordon apparently kept up their cloak-and-
dagger pretence for several days with Gordon instructed by
Booth to write a letter to Alice so that he could pass it on. In it
Gordon asked Alice whether the poison had yet arrived from
Southampton, and reassured her that she could trust Comrade
Bert 'as I could not go wrong – he knew something about me'.
This was the only testimony to indicate at what point Alice
knew Booth was in on the supposed plan.

When Booth took the letter to Alice, he met Hettie for the
first time. She was in the company of a young man, although
he was not identified. At times Booth described him as Hettie's
fiancé. The group had apparently discussed 'places of amusement' and Booth had asked whether it would be safe for him
to visit the White Hall Picture House on St Peter's Street in
Derby. Alice had warned him off, saying that there were
always soldiers in the area, and that if they were suspicious
they would ask questions that might expose him. Hettie and
her young man had then left, leaving Booth and Alice to talk
alone.

Booth said that he had then asked Alice the best way to get
a parcel through to London. She had apparently told him
either to go to the railway station in person or 'as she had

done, to get the Midland Railway van to call and ask the carman to put it on the train'. She had told Booth that 'it was safer than the bloody Post Office . . . I know from my past experience as a postmistress'. Alice had worked as a post-mistress in Bootle for a short time.

Booth claimed then to have left Pear Tree Road at 'five minutes past nine' bound for the parcel office at Derby Midland where he found a record of a package sent from Derby to 'Mason, Southampton' which had been dispatched the previous evening. Booth went again to the station on Sunday, 31 December and again on Monday, 1 January when he finally found what he was looking for – a parcel addressed to 'Mrs Wheeldon, Pear Tree Road'. With two witnesses present, the sacking and string were removed from the parcel and its contents examined. It contained 'a portion of the articles in Exhibit 20'. According to court records this was a 'green overcoat, blue jacket and grey jacket'. The green coat was identified by Booth, along with the 'collars', presumably those listed in Exhibit 19 as 'six gentlemen's collars, with different names of makes thereon'. Booth noted that there was also 'a letter' within. The package was rewrapped and sent out for delivery. Booth called at Pear Tree Road twice that day, the second time noting that Hettie, 'her fiancé' and Nellie were also in attendance.

Booth said: 'The two girls and the young man went out. After they had gone, Mrs Wheeldon said: "The poison has not arrived but I have no doubt it will if the young fellow is alive".'

At this point Alice had told Booth that the person providing the poison had once worked at Guy's Hospital in London and that this was where he had acquired it. Booth claimed not to know the identity of this person. He recalled that Alice had told him she had either seen or heard from the man just a fortnight earlier. 'I am not certain which she said,' he told the court. At this point, according to Booth, Alice had turned the conversation to Lloyd George and Arthur Henderson saying: 'I hope the buggers will soon be dead.'

Booth claimed that Alice had declared that Lloyd George had been 'the cause of millions of innocent lives being sacrificed, the bugger shall be killed to stop it . . . and as for that other bugger Henderson, he is a traitor to his people, but Asquith is the bloody brains of the business'. And then: 'Lloyd George is neither fit for heaven nor bloody hell. Another bugger that ought to be done in is George at Buckingham Palace. He has always ponced on the people and is no bloody good.' It was powerful stuff and dangerously close to calling for a revolution.

Booth remarked that at this point he had asked Alice what was the best method to poison Lloyd George, and that she had told him of a plan the Suffragettes had formulated to kill him. Booth said Alice had told him: 'We had a plan before when we spent £300 in trying to poison him . . . to get a position in a hotel where he stayed and to drive a nail through his boot that had been dipped in the poison, but he went to France, the bugger.'

Interestingly, Booth said Alice had also claimed to be part of another plot, this one to harm MP Reginald McKenna by placing a poisoned needle in a skull and sending it to his house. The plot had been abandoned because, Alice had supposedly said, 'It was argued an innocent person might touch it and die.'

Police investigations did reveal that a skull, with the words 'Votes for Women' written across its forehead, had indeed been sent to McKenna's house. Apparently neither the police nor McKenna had been informed, and only the butler and a lady's maid were aware of the skull's delivery. It was possible, then, that Alice Wheeldon had inside knowledge of the incident, although it was also quite possible that one or the other servant had later mentioned the matter to a third party. Booth, through his many contacts, could just as easily have been privy to the information. In court, very little was made of the incident.

Booth also testified that during conversations about the

poison, Alice had told Gordon: 'You know what you are doing, you will rid the world of a bloody murderer and be a saviour to the country.'

Booth stated that when asked how the poison might be administered, Alice said: 'It is a crystal and you drop two drops of water on it, dip your article in and when the water evaporates it leaves the poison.' As he left just before 9.30pm, Alice allegedly told him: 'Now look here – when I hand the poison over to you, I wash my hands of it and will deny on my word of honour that I ever gave it to you.' She had apparently also told Booth that the phial of poison would contain 'enough to kill 500'.

The following day, 2 January, Booth had again visited Alice. She had told him she was becoming concerned because the package containing the poison had not yet arrived. Booth had later gone to the railway station where another package, a cretonne-lined fish basket that had been sent by Alice to Winnie and Alf, was opened and examined.

On the afternoon of 4 January Booth returned to Alice's shop. By this time she had become quite anxious. Alice told him the package had been sent via her nephew's wife, Edith Marshall, of 187 Shaftesbury Crescent, Derby, but she had unexpectedly been away from home. Alice was concerned that the package would be returned to the 'Dead Letter Office and will be opened. It's terrible it has all the incriminating evidence in it.'

A great many witnesses from the post offices in Southampton and Derby were then called to show the jury the precise passage of the parcel. Henry Spencer, the superintendent of Derby's Midland Road Post Office, and all the members of staff who had handled the parcel gave evidence. The package had arrived at Midland Road by train and had been handed to Elizabeth Mortimer, a temporary postwoman employed as cover for regular workers who had been called up to military service. She had found no one at home at the Marshalls' and the package had been returned to the depot where Joseph Williamson, an inspector, had received it. He had passed it on to postman Walter Stoakley who had, in turn, given it to another temporary postwoman, Florence Roberts, coincidentally a near-neighbour of Edith Marshall and well acquainted with the family. Again delivery was not possible and Miss Roberts had decided to give it to Margaret Smith of 189 Shaftesbury Crescent, who had signed for it. Mrs Smith testified that she had given the parcel to Edith Marshall when she returned home around 4.30pm.

Edith, who had been visiting her husband's aunt, Alice's sister Ellen Land, at 102 Pear Tree Road, told the court that she been called on by Hettie Wheeldon, who told her that a package was expected from Winnie. When Edith had gone home to check, there had been no sign of the parcel, so she had returned to her aunt's house. Later in the day she had returned home once more, whereupon Margaret Smith had given her the parcel.

Booth's evidence also mentioned a telegram being received from Winnie advising her mother to collect the parcel from Edith Marshall. Booth stated that Hettie had gone 'down the hill' to Edith's house in search of the parcel. He had left, only to return around 7.45pm 'in the company of Gordon'. By then, the Wheeldons had possession of the missing parcel: 'Mrs Wheeldon came out of the parlour into the shop and, smiling, said: "We've got it, Hettie went down and got it . . . I've got the directions in the letter now. Will you copy it?"'

The instructions as written down by Booth on a piece of blue Hussar writing paper, but in his words 'from her dictation', were admitted as Exhibit 40. They were in a curious note form, as if someone had hurriedly written them down, although whether this was Alf Mason's style, or Booth's, is unclear. They read:

> The powder in tube A is sufficient for two or even three doses. To be given by mouth or in solution. The powder in tube C to be injected either in solution or by a dart

(which will penetrate into the body and stop for a while) rusted in solution and covered C powder from the air gun will do (walking stick gun). A rusty needle, if driven well in covered with powder rusted on etc may do, but do not advise unless in urgent dilemma. Solution B either by mouth or injection. Solution D brown injection only. All are certain A in powder form. All four will probably leave a trace but if the bloke who owns it does suspect it will be a job to prove it. As long as you have a chance to get at the dog I pity it. Dead in 20 sec. Powder A on meat or bread is ok. If you care for microbe can supply. Needle 36 hours in strong solution. Allow to dry in air, dip again for two sec. And allow again to dry. Cover with C powder.

Booth stated that Alice had then shown him a tin box containing four glass phials, all corked and sealed, and protected in cotton wool. They were marked A, B, C and D. Later scientific evidence revealed the contents of two phials to be forms of strychnine, the others types of curare.

Booth told the court that Alice said she had removed all finger-marks from the tube and the box and instructed him to wear gloves when handling it. Before they left the shop, according to Booth's account, Alice asked for his London address, which he duly supplied (102 Beverstone Road, Thornton Heath, Surrey), as she wanted him to help her secure the escape of her son, her son-in-law and another man. According to local directories, in 1917 the householder at the Thornton Heath address was one Arthur Maurice Booth.

Booth's evidence continued: 'I think she gave the box to Gordon and said: "Now don't forget if you want a microbe, send to me".' Gordon told Alice this would not be necessary and she indicated that the offer still stood, before telling him that Walton Heath 'would be the best place to catch Lloyd George with an air rifle . . . the best of luck and when you have done them in you can do the others'.

The pair left and, when they had gone some 300 yards from the property, Gordon gave the box to Booth who then drove out to meet his immediate superior, Major Lee, at the house of Charles Carwithen, the Derby postmaster. Booth handed the box and the copied instructions over to his boss.

On 13 January Alice sent a letter to 'Comrade Bert' at the address he had given her, asking about 'emigration for the boys Mac, Will & Alf. Should like to know what is being done in this direction.' She received no reply. Less than three weeks later Alice and her family were arrested.

Charles Herbert Jones, an inspector at Derby's Post Office, was next to testify. He was called upon to identify photographs of various letters sent between the defendants, all of which had been opened in transit. In a rather forlorn attempt to have the letters removed from evidence, Riza suggested that mere photographs were not admissible, and that the original letters must be produced. Justice Low refused him outright and shortly thereafter adjourned the court for lunch.

After the break the prosecution called Alfred Parry Noble, a member of staff at the Southampton town clerk's office, to testify that some of the letters were in Hettie's handwriting. Then Booth was recalled to the witness box to reiterate some details of his meetings with Alice. After this Riza began his cross-examination.

Booth told the court that he had been in the employ of the Ministry of Munitions since September 1916 and that he had 'been engaged in making certain enquiries of various organisations'. Riza pursued Booth's legal experience, asking for whom he had clerked. Booth replied: 'the late Mr Purcell'.

Riza: 'Mr Purcell was, I think, interested in criminal law?'

Much to the amusement of almost everyone in attendance, Booth retorted: 'I don't know about law, but he was interested in defending criminals. I was his clerk for seventeen years.'

If Riza's questioning had so far been ineffective, his next move was, at least, to cause a sensation in court. Journalists noted that Riza had a 'somewhat explosive manner of asking questions', which only added to the startling nature of the one he was about to pose.

'Is', Riza asked, 'the Gordon in this case Stinie Morrison?'

Stinie Morrison was notorious. He was a Russian Jewish immigrant and career criminal who had been convicted of murder after one of the most infamous cases of the century. According to newspaper reports, there was 'sensation in court' at Riza's question, perhaps for a moment in alarm that this could even be true, but more likely in sheer amazement at Riza's tactic. Booth replied that Gordon was not Stinie Morrison, while the judge wittily pointed out: 'Stinie Morrison is otherwise occupied.' Indeed he was; convicted in 1911, Morrison had been awaiting the death sentence ever since. It would not be the last the trial would hear of Stinie Morrison but, for now at least, Riza moved on.

He asked Booth what other 'secret services' he had performed but, before Booth could speak, the judge cut in: 'Don't answer.'

Riza asked Booth to describe what Gordon had told him about Alice, before the pair had been introduced. Booth replied that Gordon had said: 'She swears like a trooper,' and that he had replied: 'Then she'll do for me!' which elicited yet more laughter in court. Booth told Riza that Alice had told him she had previously possessed poison 'but she had got rid of it for fear of doing in her old man, as she was sick of him because he was a drunkard'. He also stated that poison-laced mince pies had been discussed. Under further cross-examination, Booth admitted lying about himself to Alice in order to ingratiate himself with her. Much to the disappointment of the fascinated onlookers, Booth was prevented from elaborating on the 'story of the chicken farm' by Justice Low who, according to the *Manchester Guardian*, 'nipped it in the bud'.

Booth said he had heard conversations about 'a person named McManus', and a proposed 'emigration scheme' for Will Wheeldon and Alf, and claimed that he had previously heard of McManus but knew little about him. The Attorney-

General asked Booth to expand upon this, and he replied that McManus was 'a Clyde deportee and, with another Clyde deportee, he helped to get the German hunchback, Kerhran, out of England'. This was another topic to which the court would return.

Riza suggested that Booth had also lied to the court, and that his allegation that Alice had declared Lloyd George responsible for thousands of deaths 'is a fabrication of your own mind'. Booth denied this.

Using 'pertinatious cross-examining', as the Derby press called it, Riza suggested that Alice Wheeldon was interested only in aiding the escape of certain young men from an internment camp which was guarded by dogs. Asked whether Alice wanted the poison for this purpose, Booth said she did not. And yet, by his own admission, Booth had written down directions, compiled by Alf Mason and dictated by Alice Wheeldon, and which Booth claimed were absolutely verbatim, that contained the phrase 'if you have a chance to get at the dog I pity it'. It seems unlikely that the 'dog' in question might be the Prime Minister because the paragraph also contained a reference to 'the bloke who owns it'. It is difficult to see how this might refer to a man, no matter how negatively the writer might have viewed him.

This was not a line of cross-examination that Riza chose to pursue but it would seem to be rather an important oversight on the defence counsel's part. It was a significant hole in the prosecution case and one which, had it been exposed fully, might at least have planted doubts in the jurors' minds about the true purpose of the poison.

After Riza had finished cross-examining Booth, Victor Arthur Cook, senior laboratory attendant at Hartley University College, Southampton, was called to testify, repeating the evidence he had given at Derby. He stated: 'Some months before the end of last year [1916] . . . he [Alfred Mason] gave me the curare in a green bottle [submitted as Exhibit 31], and said it was very poisonous.' Cook recalled that, over the course of several conversations, Alf had told him that if he got some of the curare in a scratch 'it would produce death very soon', but that taken internally it would be harmless. Cook stated that it had been he who had placed on the bottle a label stating: 'Curare poison. Not to be opened.' The bottle was stowed away in a cardboard box inside a cupboard. Other than removing it once to show a student, Cook stated that he had not touched the bottle. Some days before classes resumed in January, 'Mr Mason . . . asked me for the curare.' Cook testified that Alf had taken a few fragments, dissolving some in water to create a 'brown or chocolate-coloured fluid'. Alf poured this fluid into a tube and the pair sealed the cork with paraffin wax. Cook stated that he had replaced the green bottle in the cupboard and that Alf had labelled the tube with a letter of the alphabet 'but I did not see what it was'.

At the beginning of February Cook had been approached by two police detectives. He had led them to Alf's locker, on which there was no lock, and various flasks and items had been taken from there. The detectives, Cook noted, had also taken possession of the green bottle. Cook also mentioned that it was his responsibility, along with the caretaker Mr Taylor, to lock up the laboratory, but that Alf knew where the key was kept. It was still in that place when he returned to work after Christmas.

The prosecution then called its youngest witness. Fifteen-year-old Reginald Horace Pike was a junior laboratory assistant. He told the court only that Cook had talked to him about the curare, that he had seen 'Mason the lecturer' ask Cook for both the curare and a specimen tube, and that Alf 'seemed to be doing experiments with it'. It added little to Cook's evidence, but provided a great deal of fascination for the Derby newspapers. The prosecution had the young boy travel from Southampton to Derby for the hearings, and to London for the main trial. It must have been quite an adventure.

The next witness was Kathleen Tarbit, a chemistry student at Hartley University. She stated that she had attended a lecture on curare by Alf some four weeks before Christmas. She had also borrowed Alf's notebook [Exhibit 45]. There followed evidence, too, that the green bottle was not the original container of the poison. Kathleen Tarbit's fellow student Maud Nash had stated that she too had attended the curare lecture, and that this had included information about how to make it soluble. Following a subsequent lecture (she thought as early as 15 December) Alf had shown her the curare in a bottle. He had asked whether she might 'like some for my collection and I said "Yes".' Alf had then taken most of the poison from the original specimen tube and placed it in a small green bottle, handing Miss Nash the remaining poison in its original container. She had given this to Detective Inspector McCormac on 19 February. She also testified that she had asked Alf 'how he could procure the poison in this country'. He had told her a friend could supply him. She also remembered Alf telling her about a friend at Guy's Hospital, although she thought this was in relation to 'obtaining some opium'.

The origin of the curare now established, Sir Frederick's team went to great lengths, in considerable detail, to pursue the journey of the parcel into which Alf had placed the poisons, as well as a number of other packages sent in the other direction. In particular Sidney Foy, sub-postmaster at Howard Road Post Office in Southampton, just a short walk from the Masons' Millbrook Road home, said that a woman – 'I cannot describe her' – had given him a registered letter to send to 'Mrs Marshall, 187 Shaftesbury Crescent, Derby.'

Scientific evidence followed. Even at the initial hearings in Derby, there had been considerable discussion as to the nature of the substances within the mysterious phials. John Webster, assistant scientific analyst to the Home Office and a member of staff at St Mary's Hospital, Paddington, had been called upon to examine and analyse, at length, the four glass phials and their contents, finding them to be hydrochlorate of strychnine, hydrochloride of strychnine and two forms of curare. He also noted that he had been given the green glass bottle to examine and that it, too, contained curare. A bottle, Exhibit 32, entered into the records as 'Bottle used for dissolving "curare" in water', contained no trace of the poison.

To confirm and expand upon Webster's findings, Sir Frederick now called upon the imposing figure of Dr Bernard Spilsbury. A tall, immaculately groomed man in his late thirties, Spilsbury had already established a reputation as the pre-eminent expert in the new science of forensics and, in particular, toxicology. Spilsbury had testified as an expert witness in a number of high-profile cases, most notably the trial of Dr Hawley Harvey Crippen in 1910, and in Sir Archibald Bodkin's star turn, the Brides in the Bath Murders. His appearance at the Wheeldon trial would only add to his fame. That the Attorney-General had chosen such a distinguished expert to assist his case is unsurprising. Spilsbury was *the* authority on such matters and was becoming something of an audience-pleaser in his own right. His presence could only have impressed still further on the minds of the jury the importance and severity of the charges.

At the Derby hearing Spilsbury had made a statement about the dangers of the two poisons, their effects, the symptoms of those effects and possible ways of administering them. He had also elaborated on the origins and exotic nature of curare and noted that it was not widely available, but was 'procurable from certain firms of wholesale druggists by recognised scientific men . . . the hospital laboratories usually possess it'. At the Old Bailey, too, Spilsbury described the effects of curare on humans in some detail. He could not, however, be certain of what the minimum fatal dose would be. Sir Archibald Bodkin asked Spilsbury whether the instructions that had been read out in court the previous day, for the use of the poison, were accurate. He replied that they were.

Under cross-examination Spilsbury admitted that he did not know of a single example 'in scientific literature' of curare being administered by a dart. Riza asked Spilsbury whether it wasn't the case that Sir Walter Raleigh had introduced curare [to Britain] in 1595. The judge noted: 'I don't think the witness was alive then.' Again Riza's flow was interrupted and the court dissolved into laughter. Riza then asked whether curare was an antidote to strychnine. It was not. He took an arrow from a bundle and passed it to Spilsbury, asking him whether he knew anything about such weapons. Spilsbury said he had seen similar items. Riza cautioned him not to touch the point, but Spilsbury replied: 'Oh, I do not think there is much poison on this one.'

Justice Low asked Riza whether he wanted the dart. Riza replied that he 'might want it later', and Justice Low again caused much laughter in the court by replying: 'Then you had better keep it until you do want it.' Spilsbury's testimony ended with confirmation that it was theoretically possible to poison a man by driving a nail dipped in poison through the sole of his boot.

At this point the prosecution called Major William Lauriston Lee. A former army man, now employed by the Ministry of Munitions, Lee was Booth's immediate superior. He had been involved in the investigations into several agitators, among them Willie Paul. In his original statement, Lee had told the Derby court: 'There is a Mr Booth, an enquiry agent of that Department [within the Ministry of Munitions]. He engages others to assist him. Alec [*sic*] Gordon was one he engaged.' His testimony dealt mainly with details of the opening and examining of parcels at the Post Office in Derby, and of the copying of some of the contents. In particular he testified that on the evening of 4 January Booth had met him and handed him the tin of poisons, plus the paper on which he had written the dictated instructions. The following day he had taken the box to Scotland Yard, where he had given it to Inspector Parker.

Letters intercepted by the Post Office at Lee's request were discussed. Among them was a letter from Winnie to her mother, written on 3 January. Among myriad topics discussed, Winnie suggested a number of books her mother might enjoy. One of them was *A Bed of Roses* by 'W. Lloyd George'. There was great amusement in court when it transpired that Winnie had noted: 'No relation, thank God.' In fact Winnie had made a mistake; the author was Walter Lionel George, a writer on feminism with a strong anti-war stance, but if they were aware of the error, Bodkin and Lee made sure not to let it spoil a good joke.

Riza restored order and seriousness to the proceedings with his cross-examination. He asked Lee whether he had met Gordon. Lee replied that he had not. Riza asked whether Lee could reveal Gordon's location. Lee replied that it was 'no affair of mine', a smart reply that earned a rebuke from the judge, who told Lee: 'The answer is "No".' And then, in a rare moment of sympathy for the defence, he told Riza: 'Do not hesitate, Mr Riza, to put any questions which may further the interests of your case.'

Riza asked Lee if he knew whether Gordon had a criminal record. Sidestepping the issue entirely, Lee replied: 'I have already explained to you that I do not know the man. I cannot answer questions on matters beyond my own knowledge.' Riza asked why Lee had gone to Derby, and the witness replied that he had 'employed Booth to get into touch with people who might be likely to commit sabotage'.

A number of less dramatic witness accounts were then heard. Derby photographer Thomas Wallis, who had business premises on Sadler Gate, told the court that he had been required to take photographs of certain documents and letters at the request of Lee's subordinate, Frederick De Valda; Malcolm Brodie, a lieutenant attached to the General Post Office in London, testified that handwriting on a telegram was the same as that on a form filled out by Winnie in Southampton; and Charles Carwithen gave his account of the interception of various letters between the defendants, their examination by Major Lee and the photography of the items.

Inspector Higham of the Derby Borough Police gave details of items found on the defendants at the time of their arrests. Riza asked Higham about some slips of paper bearing the words 'Taffy was a Welshman' and a song entitled, 'We'll hang Lloyd George on a sour apple tree'. After some amusement at this in court, Higham replied that the phrases were used as 'tests for the code'.

The testimony of Albert Foyer, a code expert from the GPO, explained the contents of several letters. One was from Alf to Alice and included a coded section that revealed his plans. The translated section read: 'Dear Ma, Am cycling to Derby, starting from here early Saturday morning. Hope to be in Liverpool on Monday to try for dispensing crib on a liner arriving in the evening if all goes well. All our letters are opened, am informed by a post office official. Don't send anything incriminating openly.'

It was, of course, hardly surprising that the Masons and Wheeldons were attempting to conceal their activities. Even plans to assist COs, or an attempt by Alf to avoid his call-up, needed to be kept out of the sight of the authorities.

The prosecution ended its case by pre-empting the defence. Sir Frederick called Major Edward Gibbs Kimber to the witness box to make a statement regarding the accuseds' claims that they intended to use the poison to incapacitate dogs guarding CO internment camps. Kimber replied that no dogs were used at such camps.

Chapter 8

Nothing but a Coincidence

When Saiyid Riza called his first witness for the defence, there was considerable anticipation. And Alice Wheeldon did not disappoint when she refused to swear on the Bible. The judge remarked: 'You say that an affirmation will be the only power binding upon your conscience?' It was a question loaded with the implication that the witness, by refusing to swear to God, might be less inclined to full honesty, but she was defiant. Yet if the prosecution was hoping that Alice, whom they had thus far painted as an angry, uncouth woman, would come across as a firebrand, or as an angry revolutionary, it was they who were to be disappointed now. Under examination by Riza, she spoke very quietly, so quietly indeed that the barrister had to make repeated requests for her to speak up.

Alice explained how she had first met both Gordon and Booth; she claimed that they had told her that dogs now guarded the camps in which conscientious objectors were held; and that they had suggested to her that poison would be necessary to eliminate the animals. She told the court that she had informed the men that her son-in-law, Alf Mason, was a chemist and that he could help obtain the poison. This, of course, was in absolute contrast to the testimony of Booth, who had claimed that Alice had not told him the identity of the person who could supply the poison. Significantly, it was also different from what she had told Winnie and Alf themselves. In a letter of 2 January, only two days before the arrival of the poison, Alice had written of Gordon, although not by name, that 'he does not know you exist'.

Alice also claimed to have told Gordon that Alf was liable for military service and that the pair had also discussed police dogs. She explained that her interest in Gordon and Booth was solely in their talk of escaping military service. She said: 'The thing that most interested me was emigration. I wanted to get three CO boys across to America.'

At this point Alice was less than forthcoming with the truth. She claimed that Gordon had told her about a man named Swayze and another named McManus who could help 'so as to get them across'. In court, as she had to the two agents, Alice had neglected to mention her familiarity with Arthur McManus. Quite why she had done this is unclear; Alice's testimony now identified McManus as someone willing to help COs escape, and she had done little to protect her ally. She now said:

> Being a businesswoman I made a bargain with him [Gordon] that if I could assist him in getting his friends from a concentration camp by getting rid of the dogs, he would, in his turn, see to the three boys, my son, Mason and a young man named MacDonald, whom I have kept, get away.

Alice claimed this conversation had taken place on 25 December, although Booth had suggested the first contact had taken place on the 27th of that month.

Gordon, Alice said, had given her 'some particulars about his past experiences', that he had 'posed in London as an Indian for three months, and also pretended to be deaf and dumb'. Alice confirmed that she had told Gordon he should stay away from her house, as Booth had stated, but that this was because her husband 'did not like COs'.

Riza asked Alice whether she had done anything 'in the furtherance of that bargain'. Alice responded that she had written 'to my daughter Winnie at Southampton on 1 January'. She told the court that Booth, as Comrade Bert, had brought a note from Gordon, 'but I cannot produce it, I burnt it. As far as I can remember the note said: "Trust Bert implicitly. You can place full confidence in him. Burn this as soon as you get it. I will do the same with your communication". The note was signed Alex Gordon.'

Riza asked whether the note had made any reference to the bargain. It did not, she said. Alice could not recall whether she saw Booth again that day, but said that Gordon had written a letter of introduction to Arthur McManus on behalf of Alice and her 'boys'.

Justice Low reminded Riza that 'what counsel referred to as the emigration scheme was not very material to this case'. That was certainly true, as Alice's involvement in the 'emigration scheme' did nothing to prove or disprove the prosecution's case that she was planning to poison the Prime Minister. What it did do was support Alice's assertion that she had been drawn in by Gordon and Booth because of their apparent sympathy to the plight of her son, her son-in-law and her young friend.

Alice described receiving a telegram from Southampton on 4 January. This had been admitted as Exhibit 46 and concerned the missing poison parcel. It had been sent to 'Mrs Wheeldon' by Winnie in Southampton at 9.47am, and had arrived at the Derby telegram office just over an hour later. Its message was simple: 'Call at Edies [*sic*], if nothing wire.' As a result, Alice 'sent Hettie to go down to . . . Shaftesbury Crescent that evening'.

Later, when Gordon and Booth visited her shop, Alice told them that the poison had arrived, and that it had been delivered via Mrs Marshall: 'I had opened the box which contained the bottles and a letter of instructions from Winnie to me. The letter was about my boys' trip to America.'

Justice Low then asked: 'Was there anything about poison?'

Alice replied: 'Yes, about poison for the dogs.'

The judge again: 'Do you remember taking anything down from dictation?' To this Alice replied that she had given the instructions to use the poison 'into Booth's hands'.

Justice Low: 'Were they in the letter?'

Alice: 'No.'

Justice Low: 'Then there were two documents in the box?'

Alice: 'Yes.'

Justice Low: 'You did not tell us that. You say one letter was written by Winnie. Who was the other written by?'

Alice: 'The directions about the poison were written by my son-in-law Mason.'

The judge asked Alice whether she could remember anything of the instructions. She replied that Alf had noted that the poison was dangerous, and that 'it was necessary to get near the dogs to destroy then. He said they had to be very careful.' Riza then asked Alice: 'What use did you make of the poison?'

Alice: 'I handed it to Gordon.'

Riza: 'What happened to the paper on which the instructions were written?'

Alice: 'I handed it to Bert and asked him to make notes.'

Booth had alleged that Alice had read the note out to him. When asked by the judge what had happened to the original instructions, Alice replied that she had burnt them because she had 'promised Gordon that nobody should know anything about it but myself'.

The judge then asked Alice to read a passage from a letter she had written to Winnie and Alf on 2 January, which Alice duly did: 'Will you send me that stuff? I want it for a fellow who will risk anything to accomplish something.' It was all fairly non-specific. Had the prosecution chosen to call Alex Gordon to the witness box, Alice might have found herself questioned about another letter she supposedly sent to her son-in-law. In one of his reports to the Ministry of Munitions, Gordon claimed that Alice had packed up a parcel containing various foods and gifts. Among the items enclosed were four mince pies. It was later revealed that this parcel was bound for the Masons. According to Gordon's report: 'In the centre of one of the pies was a note addressed to "Dear A", and signed "Z", asking for the phial of poison to be sent at once, as a man had been found who would remove "L George" if at all possible.' No such pie-stained note was found and no evidence regarding this incident was brought before the court. But the letter, from which the judge had just asked Alice to read, had included the question: 'Did you get the pie paper?'

Without the actual note to examine, we can never be certain of the words written upon it. But if it existed, and Alice's own words certainly suggest that it did, then we can be sure that a very important secret message was passing between the two households. Whether this referred to a plot to poison a prime minister can never be known.

Alice then stated that she had promised her daughter that she would not implicate her husband. In fact, in the letter she had written she promised: 'It will not implicate anyone who belongs to us.'

The judge asked Alice whether this referred only to her 'efforts to get Jews out of the court'. She replied: 'Yes.'

The third day of the trial was held up because one of the jurymen had been taken ill with influenza. Riza was called to the judge's box and then visited the cells to consult with his clients. The court assembled at 11.10am when the judge announced that they would shortly be hearing the evidence of a medical expert, and expected to learn that the sick juror would be incapacitated for some considerable time. He told the court that he had two choices. He could either adjourn the case indefinitely until such time as the juror was able to return, or he could restart the trial with a new juryman in place. Clearly Justice Low preferred the latter option since delaying matters was not 'in the public interest or in the interest of the prisoners to accept'.

Addressing the jury, Justice Low noted: 'This is a charge that certainly ought to be disposed of as soon as conveniently may be, and not kept hanging about or impending over the heads of the prisoners. I think, gentlemen, you will probably agree.' Several jurymen indicated they did. The Attorney-General was in agreement too, but Riza preferred that the case be continued with only the eleven remaining jurors since beginning from scratch would subject his clients 'to a severe ordeal'.

Justice Low reminded Riza that, under English law, twelve jurors must be used. When the evidence of the juror's doctor confirmed their fears, the judge agreed with the jurors to convene an hour earlier each day for the remainder of the trial.

With the new juryman sworn in, the whole process began once more with counsel repeating their questions, and witnesses their evidence.

There were, however, occasional additions. Victor Cook, Alf's lab assistant, added that Alf had not told him that the curare he was putting in the bottle was to be used on dogs at internment camps. When Hiscock of the Southampton Post Office gave evidence, Riza decided to cross-examine him on the handwriting of a certain letter. The judge tried to stop him, noting that eleven jurors had heard Alice talk about the letter the previous day, and that the twelfth man would soon hear her testimony, rendering the entire cross-examination pointless. Riza argued that he had forgotten to ask a pertinent question and the judge chided: 'It is very unfortunate that you allowed your client to leave the box without raising the question of the letter.' Riza noted that, as far as this witness was concerned, this would be the only letter he would contest and the case moved on for the rest of the day.

The fourth day saw a change of location, with the trial at last moved to the much larger no. 1 Court. More witnesses were recalled, many of whom had been forced, yet again, to travel up from Southampton or Derby. The case for the Crown was completed just 40 minutes into the day and the judge noted with satisfaction: 'You have finished five minutes sooner than I thought.'

Once more the defence began with Alice's testimony and Justice Low again chose to debate with Alice the rights and wrongs of her decision to affirm, rather than swear upon the Bible. This time Alice surprised the court by stating that she was a Quaker and that this meant she could not swear on the Bible.

Evidence from her first statement was repeated. Alice stated that Gordon had told her that he knew of at least thirty COs who had escaped to America, and that he was particularly interested in 'five Yiddish still in the concentration camp'. They had apparently discussed the 'hunchback Kerhran', the same man that Booth had mentioned in his testimony. Gordon had claimed to have helped him to escape, along with 'Swayze'. Both men were, it seemed, Jewish.

Kerhran's name had come up in a letter to Winnie, posted in Derby on 9 January. The correspondent of this letter, although unidentified by the authorities, was almost certainly Alexander Mann MacDonald, the young CO who had been discovered at Alice's shop on the day of her arrest. The writer told Winnie that, although 'the Boys spent several hours in faking him up, that hump was his undoing, he was spotted, brought back, and handed over'. His discovery had led to McManus and the others having to 'lie low, and our Heave "O" on the saline solution is postponed'. In other words, they would have to wait before seeking passage on a liner. In a report to the Ministry of Munitions around this time, Alex Gordon had described an encounter with MacDonald, who had just returned from a meeting with McManus in Liverpool, and who had recounted to him a very similar story.

Alice claimed that when she had told Gordon that her son-in-law was a chemist, he had asked her whether she might be able to help. Gordon told her: 'We can buy the gun but not the poison.' At this point, she said, Gordon had asked whether Alf could get the necessary poison to incapacitate the dogs. Riza asked Alice whether she had replied. She told him that she had agreed to see 'what could be done'. Again Alice explained why she was prepared to do this: 'I said I was willing to make a bargain and if he would help my son to get away to America I would undertake to get the poison for the dogs.'

The examination then turned to Alice's meetings with Booth. She denied that several of the alleged conversations had even taken place – in particular the one about a stuffed snakeskin bracelet, and Booth's allegation that she had expressed a desire to have 'a hundred of them'.

Riza then moved on to her comments about Reuben Farrow, the Christian Socialist NCF man. Riza asked Alice to clarify the meaning of her comments about his 'milk and water Jesus Christ methods'. Alice stated that she and Farrow disagreed over 'the Home Office scheme for alternative service', which she believed to be just another form of conscription.

Alice then stated that Booth had known about the poison because Gordon had told him. Riza asked her whether she had, as Booth had alleged, expressed concerns that the missing parcel must have gone to the Dead Letter Office and that she was afraid all the incriminating evidence would be discovered. Alice, shaking her head, said: 'I am doubtful if I did say so.'

Alice stated once more that, once the parcel had been collected, she had placed it on her shop counter and, in the presence of both Gordon and Booth, had unpacked it. She confirmed again the prosecution's details of what was inside the parcel, and that Booth had made his own copy of the instructions.

The judge then put some of his own questions, in particular about Booth's allegation that Alice had suggested supplying a microbe if required. Alice replied that, yes, she did understand that a microbe was a 'disease germ' and had 'known that for many years'. Justice Low asked if it struck Alice 'as a good thing to use in killing a dog which was about to attack?' Alice replied: 'It sounds ridiculous.' The judge agreed. Alice denied that she had offered a microbe to Booth, and also that any further conversation on the subject had taken place. She also vehemently denied telling Booth that Walton Heath would be the best place to attack the Prime Minister and that no other person had made that suggestion either. In testament to the honesty of her principles, Alice did admit making a great many derisive comments about Lloyd George, Asquith and the King. But she stated clearly that Booth had never asked her about the best way to kill the Prime Minister, and she denied ever telling Booth that, as part of the Suffragette movement, she had knowledge of an abandoned plan to place a poisoned nail in Lloyd George's boot.

Far from attempting to conceal her beliefs, Alice Wheeldon was comfortable in asserting her convictions. But her brazen honesty was in danger of turning the jury against her, regardless of any evidence. There was near uproar in court when she admitted telling Booth that she hoped Lloyd George and Arthur Henderson would soon be dead; that she had 'said it often' and that it had 'represented her wish'. She was certain, though, that she had not said that as she handed over the poison to Gordon.

The Attorney-General himself then resumed his cross-examination. He began by making Alice agree that her answers to the previous cross-examination were still her chosen answers. Over the course of her two stints in the witness box, Alice freely admitted having done everything she could to assist fugitives from the armed forces, regardless of whether a tribunal had ruled them a CO or not, and explained that she had never knowingly turned such a person away. During the first examination Justice Low asked Alice whether she had ever 'troubled to find out whether the objections were conscientious or not'. Alice replied that she thought they 'would not go through these trials if they were not'.

When questioned on the subject of her son Will, Alice became quite emotional. She cried as she told Sir Frederick that he had been sent to prison for 18 months. Sir Frederick asked her once more to describe her attitude to the Prime Minister: 'Have you a strong feeling against ministers responsible for these acts, and in particular against Mr Lloyd George?'

Alice: 'Yes.'
Sir Frederick: 'You regard him as a traitor to the labouring classes?'
Alice: 'Yes.'

The judge then had to warn the onlookers that their accompanying ripples of laughter must not be repeated.

When the Attorney-General pointed out that Alice was somewhat indecisive and in something of an awkward position, pleading not guilty in court to plotting to murder a man she had, by her own admission, stated many times ought to be dead, Alice replied in a stinging, defiant tone: 'My position does not affect my opinion.'

Sir Frederick said: 'You are very frank. And you are not sure that you don't think he ought to be killed now?' Alice hesitated, apparently cautious that she was about to be drawn into a trap by the question. Demanding an answer Sir Frederick loudly said 'What?' and Alice replied, equally loudly, 'No, I am not!' Then Sir Frederick asked Alice about some of the unpleasant epithets she had attached to Lloyd George's name.

> Justice Low: 'Do you always talk like that?'
>   Alice: 'I have done recently.'
>   Sir Frederick: 'Ever since you became a Quaker?'

At this there was more amusement in court, provoking Justice Low to comment, 'No, no we don't want that sort of thing!'

Alice admitted that she had probably said that she wanted Lloyd George and Henderson dead; it was something she was likely to say. Sir Frederick asked her whether she had also stated that the King should be killed. She admitted that she had, and that she 'meant it at the time in bitterness'. When asked whether she still held that opinion, Alice replied only, 'I refuse to answer.'

During her second examination Alice conceded that her comments about Lloyd George and Henderson might be interpreted as something of a threat. Sir Frederick asked whether, supposing that the men were to be killed, poison would not be just as appropriate to enable their deaths as it would the deaths of dogs?

> Alice: 'Well, it would if their death were decided. I did not desire the threat should be carried out.'
>   Smith: 'But you said they ought to be killed?'
>   Alice: 'I have said so frequently.'
>   Justice Low: 'You have admitted it.'

The Attorney-General then reminded Alice of her first cross-examination and her refusal to state whether she still thought Lloyd George and Henderson should be killed. 'You still decline to answer?' Alice replied 'Yes.' At this, the judge reminded Smith: 'She is entitled to decline.'

Smith moved on. Alice told him that she had not thought to suggest to Gordon that he could obtain the poison for himself. The judge stepped in: 'It did not suggest itself to you that to obtain poison at Southampton, post it to Derby and send it

back to London to poison police dogs was an odd proceeding?'
'No,' replied Alice.

Then came Smith's most loaded question yet: 'Was it that
you had a conscientious objection to the shedding of blood
that you thought Mr Lloyd George ought to be killed?' Either
Alice was not concerned how her answer would be interpreted, or she simply did not see the trap coming: 'I have said
so many times.'

This time the judge beat the Attorney-General to the post:
'That is a bloodthirsty expression to come from one who has a
conscientious objection to the taking of human life.' There was
simply no answer Alice could give to explain the contradictions
of her stance, and Riza's re-examination was short, asking
Alice whether those to whom she had expressed her feelings
for the Prime Minister, those with whom she was politically
allied, shared her opinions. Alice answered that they did.

The judge then asked a few more questions of his own about
Alice's comments at the time of her arrest:

> Justice Low: 'When you were arrested and told you
> would be charged with conspiracy to murder, of
> course such a terrible charge must have considerably
> surprised you?'
>   Alice: 'It did.'
> Justice Low: 'Your reply was: "I know nothing about
> it." Why did you not say: "Bless my soul. I never meant
> to kill people at all, it was only dogs"?'
>   Alice: 'I was too taken aback to say anything at all.'
> Justice Low: 'But you did say something. You said
> you knew nothing about it.'

The judge pointed out that since, by the time of the police court,
Alice fully understood the nature and severity of the charges
against her, she could then have told the magistrates that she
only intended to harm dogs. Alice admitted that she could offer
no reasonable answer as to why she had not done so.

And with that, Alice Wheeldon's time in the witness box came to an end.

Hettie was next to give evidence. According to the *Derby Daily Telegraph*:

> From the dock to the witness box she walked across the well of the court with that confidence that characterised her demeanour from the first. Most of the replies given to her counsel were jerked out in a half-defiant tone. It was when the learned judge intervened, as he did frequently, that the words of the witness were uttered in a low key, and often travelled scarcely beyond the witness box, so that in some parts of the court observers rose from their seats to catch the answers.

Hettie, too, chose to affirm, this time as an atheist.

She conceded there had been frequent conversations at 12 Pear Tree Road about Lloyd George, and that there had been talk of harming him. However, these had only been hypothetical or philosophical. At no point did she suggest that her mother had been present, nor that any plan for actually killing Lloyd George had been formulated.

In fact Hettie stated that it had been Gordon and Booth who had suggested the idea and that she disagreed with them wholeheartedly: 'I said I thought assassination was ridiculous. The only thing to be done was to organise the men in the workshops against compulsory military service. I said assassination was ridiculous because if you killed one you would have to kill another and so it would go on.'

Riza then revealed his reasons for his surprise question to Booth about the murderer Stinie Morrison. Hettie had, it seemed, discussed a wide range of topics with Booth and Gordon. Riza asked: 'Was anything said about Stinie Morrison by Gordon or Booth?' Hettie replied: 'Yes, we were talking about Anarchists. He [Gordon] said Stinie Morrison put an "s" on the dead man's forehead by orders. I asked if Morrison was in prison and Gordon said: "No." I then asked Gordon: "Where is Stinie Morrison?" and he answered: "I don't know".'

When questioned about the need to encode some portions of their private letters, Hettie told the court that the cipher was used only to disguise names and conceal any mention of their 'emigration scheme'. She then said that one of her letters to Winnie, brought as evidence, had been written in regard to a man having been killed by the military. 'His kit weighed more than he did,' she noted. Her letter about the 'Darlington mutiny', in which she had told her sister, '5 officers have been killed. Cannot get to know more, naturally. Wish it would spread,' was intended only to show how bad the discontent had become, but her apparent dispassion at the deaths did little to further her cause.

Hettie stated that a comment about Lloyd George's visit to the Pope in Rome simply reflected her opinion that he might be shot at there. The judge interrupted to note: 'You wrote: "He may be seeing His Majesty soon".' Hettie explained that she was not referring to the King, but to 'the Almighty'. According to newspaper reports, this surprised the judge, and Hettie reminded him that such a reference might 'be blasphemy in the mind of a Christian, but I am not one'. At this point the Attorney-General drew attention to Hettie's employment as a schoolteacher where, among other 'secular subjects', she had taught Scripture and the Gospels for seven years, despite her self-confessed atheism.

On the subject of her opposition to the war, Hettie told Smith that it was not this specific war, nor her country's involvement in it, to which she objected, but all war. As to her knowledge of the supposed plot, Hettie was vehement that she knew nothing about the proposed use of poison, or the fact that her mother had obtained any for Gordon. The first time she had been aware of the possibility was at the police court in Derby.

Hettie then told the court that she had been instantly suspicious of her mother's new confidants: 'I thought Gordon and

Booth were police spies. I told my mother of my suspicions on 28 December. By the following Monday [1 January] I was satisfied they were spies. I then said to my mother: "You can do what you like, but I am having nothing to do with it".'

> Sir Frederick: 'Did you think your mother might be led into a trap?'
> Hettie: 'Yes.'
> Sir Frederick: 'You would have nothing to do with it because you believed the two men were spies?'
> Hettie: 'That was one reason.'

What other reasons Hettie might have given to avoid contact with the pair remained undisclosed because the Attorney-General moved on to the subject of a telegram sent from Winnie in Southampton to Pear Tree Road, querying the non-arrival of the parcel containing the poison.

'I am', he said, 'testing the credibility of your story, and I ask you what impression was produced on your mind by the receipt of that telegram at Derby?' According to the *Derby Daily Telegraph*, Hettie replied airily: 'Oh nothing extraordinary.' And that was probably the case; the telegram had been a very simple instruction to call at Edith Marshall's house, and if nothing had arrived then to wire the Masons.

There seemed little evidence to link Hettie with the supposed plot. But the Attorney-General was determined to cast doubt on her character at least. He moved on to a letter Hettie had written to her sister in which she had discussed the likelihood of further Zeppelin raids and the probability of illness spreading throughout those sheltering from the raids. Of particular interest was the assertion: 'If many spend the night in the cellar, there'll be a plague of pneumonia. Still it will serve them right what they get.' It was an unfortunate turn of phrase because the recent Zeppelin raids had been highly destructive and terrifying. Hettie denied that she had meant any harm by her comments and said that the raids were 'a bad thing'.

Nevertheless, the judge asked: 'But you seem to put it as a good thing and it is a curious view from a person who objects to bloodshed.' The Attorney-General followed up: 'Were you pleased at the prospect?' Hettie answered: 'I simply stated a fact.'

After some sparring between witness and judge, Hettie did admit that, while she would not derive any satisfaction from such an event occurring, she did believe that the people would get their due for their actions. When the Attorney-General asked Hettie to tell that to the jury – the twelve representatives of the 'people' in question – she stated she would 'think about it' and then attempted to clarify her opinions: 'I was not pleased or satisfied. I simply said they must stand by the consequences.'

> Attorney-General: 'If the English people sheltered from Zepps and there was a plague of pneumonia, they would get their deserts – that is your view?'
> Hettie: 'Yes.'
> Attorney-General: 'You also wrote: "Who can blame the Germans now for taking their revenge on rhinoceros-skinned, perfidious, and canting Britain?" Was that your opinion of your country?'

After a little encouragement from the judge, Hettie confirmed that this was the case, and that she still held that view.

Then came general questions about comments she had made in another letter about the Clyde engineers and various industrial revolts in the north before Justice Low returned to Hettie's letter about Lloyd George's visit to Rome. He asked whether the words 'pray without sneezing' was a slang expression for 'pray without ceasing'. Hettie said it was not. In his later re-examination, Riza asked Hettie to clarify this, and she said that it was simply 'a common joke' in her circle. The judge was appalled by her answer, telling Hettie: 'It seems a horrible thing for a girl like you to be coupling an expression of jocularity with somebody's death.' Hettie said that she had meant 'practically nothing' by it.

During the remaining cross-examination, Justice Low asked whether Hettie's reference to Lloyd George soon meeting God might refer to his death. Hettie said that it did.

> Justice Low: 'Consider this then. You have written a letter speaking about the death of Mr Lloyd George, and apparently anticipating it with satisfaction, a few days before a box has been received into the house in which you were living, containing four violent poisons. Can you give any explanation of what is apparently a coincidence?'
>
> Hettie: 'I can give no explanation whatever, except that it is a coincidence. He was going over to France, and I thought he might be shot. Public men are liable to be assassinated.'
>
> Low: 'Does not the reference to praying mean praying for that result?'
>
> Hettie: 'No, it is nothing but a coincidence.'
>
> Low: 'It seems to me to be an unfortunate coincidence.'
>
> Hettie: 'Yes, it is for me.'

The Attorney-General then put it to Hettie that she had been in her 'mother's confidence throughout'. Hettie denied this, stating firmly: 'I have never been taken into my mother's confidence and know nothing whatever about this charge.'

Throughout her evidence, Hettie Wheeldon was steadfast in maintaining her own innocence of the charges, yet entirely comfortable with revealing the depths and details of her political and moral beliefs. Her fate relied on the jurors being able, or willing, to distinguish between the two.

Winnie Mason's arrival in the witness box was recorded only briefly in the late news column of the *Derby Daily Telegraph*, and in little more detail in the weekly *Derby Mercury*, where

The spark that ignited the First World War: Gavrilo Princip is taken into custody after assassinating Archduke Franz Ferdinand in Sarajevo in June 1914. (*Illustrated London News Picture Library*)

Left: Under the fatherly eye of the recruiting sergeants, men from all walks of life flocked to enlist when Britain declared war on Germany in August 1914. (*Author's collection*)

Right: A government poster campaign urged waverers to answer the call to serve King and Country. (*Author's collection*)

The grim reality: blinded Allied troops at a casualty clearing station on the Western Front. (*Author's collection*)

Injured soldiers and their nurses pictured at the Derbyshire Royal Infirmary in 1915. (*Author's collection*)

The war comes to Derby: damage to the engine shed at the town's railway works after the German Zeppelin raid on 31 January 1916. (*Author's collection*)

Conscientious objectors pictured at Dyce camp, situated at a quarry works near Aberdeen, in October 1916. (*Leeds University Library*)

THE WOMEN WHO WILL ORGANISE THE NATION'S WOMEN.—See Page 3.

DAILY SKETCH.

GUARANTEED DAILY NETT SALE MORE THAN 1,000,000 COPIES.

No. 2,465.   LONDON, THURSDAY, FEBRUARY 1, 1917.   [Registered as a Newspaper.]   ONE HALFPENNY.

THE LLOYD GEORGE MURDER PLOT.

Mrs. Wheeldon.

The arrest of Mrs. Wheeldon by Chief Inspector Parker, of Scotland Yard.
—(Daily Sketch Photograph.)

Mrs. Mason, Mrs. Wheeldon's daughter.

Hetty, Mrs. Wheeldon's daughter.

A. G. Mason, Mrs. Mason's husband.

Mr. Arthur Henderson.

Mrs. Wheeldon

Mrs. Mason   Hetty Wheeldon   A. G. Mason

The accused in Court.—(Daily Sketch Photograph.)

Mr. Lloyd George.

Further details of the alleged conspiracy—first made public in news and pictures by the *Daily Sketch*—to murder Mr. Lloyd George and Mr. Arthur Henderson were revealed at Derby yesterday, when Mrs. Alice Wheeldon, Hetty Wheeldon, her daughter, Winnie Mason, her married daughter, and A. G. Mason, her son-in-law, were formally charged and remanded.

Front page of the *Daily Sketch* on 1 February 1917, reporting the first day of the sensational trial that had opened in Derby. (*John Frost Historic Newspapers*)

Alice Wheeldon (right) pictured at Derby Guildhall during the committal hearing. Next to her are her daughters, Winnie Mason (right) and Hettie Wheeldon. The woman on the extreme left is a prison wardress. (*Mary Evans Picture Library*)

Below: No. 12 Pear Tree Road, Derby, pictured in 2008 when it was the home of a mortgage broker. Some ninety years earlier it was the focal point of the nation, the home of Alice Wheeldon, who from here sold second-hand clothes and gave comfort to conscientious objectors. (*Author's collection*)

Right: Alf Mason, Winnie's husband, a chemist who was accused of procuring poison with which to murder Lloyd George. (*Mary Evans Picture Library*)

Derby Guildhall.
(*Author's collection*)

The scene inside Derby Guildhall during the committal proceedings. (*Mary Evans Picture Library*)

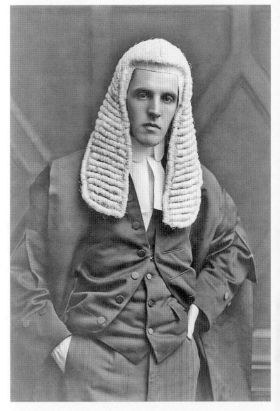

Attorney-General Sir Frederick Smith.
(*US Library of Congress/Bain News Service*)

Arthur McManus, a vociferous anti-conscription and anti-war campaigner, who married Hettie Wheeldon. (*Author's collection*)

Tom Bell, another anti-war campaigner; he regularly visited Alice Wheeldon. (*Author's collection*)

Emmeline Pankhurst is carried away from Buckingham Palace. The Suffragette leader distanced her organisation from the Wheeldons' alleged murder plot. (*Author's collection*)

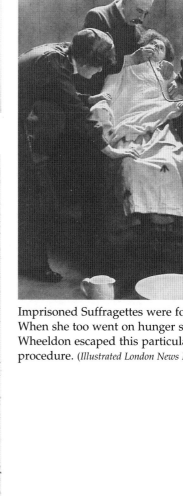

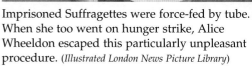

Imprisoned Suffragettes were force-fed by tube. When she too went on hunger strike, Alice Wheeldon escaped this particularly unpleasant procedure. (*Illustrated London News Picture Library*)

The government spy Alex Gordon, also known as William Rickard or Francis Vivien. (*British Library*)

her accent was described as 'rather more refined'. Unlike her mother and elder sister, the former regular churchgoer Winnie had chosen to take the oath 'in the usual way'. She admitted readily having helped her mother obtain poison, but insisted that it was for 'some dogs'. She said that she had not been particularly curious about the nature of the dogs concerned and had not asked her mother for further details, imagining simply 'a very dangerous dog', although the *Derby Daily Telegraph* account did say that she knew it was 'part of the scheme for liberating prisoners from internment'. Indeed, in a letter of 4 January, in which she mentioned the parcel of poison, Winnie had closed with the phrase: 'I do hope its all right abaht them things for the dawg.'

Winnie also admitted that she had asked her husband about the use of poison in walking sticks and air guns. She was asked about the tone of a number of her letters and noted that in 'her circle' comments about Lloyd George were often made, just as those opposing them might make comments against conscientious objectors. She agreed with the judge that, in one letter: 'Circumstantially it looks black.'

The judge asked whether anyone had suggested that the Prime Minister be poisoned. Winnie said that this had not been the case. When the Attorney-General asked Winnie whether she held her mother's views, she replied that she did not, and that she had not 'for the last two or three years'. Sir Frederick then asked why her brother could not simply purchase the poison required to kill dogs from a local chemist. He could just as well have asked why Winnie, Hettie or Alice could not purchase the poison, but perhaps it proved useful at this point to remind the jury of Winnie's imprisoned CO brother. Winnie replied that 'the existing restrictions' meant that her brother would have been quite unable to obtain such poisons. Substantiating evidence for this had come from the prosecution's own expert, Dr Spilsbury, who had declared that such poisons were obtainable from wholesalers only by 'recognised scientific men'.

Winnie then testified that her husband had 'poisoned dogs for years'. Sir Frederick drew the witness's attention to a letter that, in the words of the *Derby Daily Telegraph*, had contained 'some vile epithets applied to the Prime Minister and an awful form of curse'. There was certainly no shortage of these, Winnie having called Lloyd George on one occasion 'that buggering Welsh sod'. After Justice Low had asked Winnie to remind the court of her tender age, she said that the letter had been nothing more than a way of letting off steam; it had been 'a safety valve'.

Unfortunately for Winnie, Alf Mason's testimony implied that her involvement in the scheme to free COs was less vague than she herself might have suggested. Giving his evidence 'much as he would have addressed a class at college, leaning forward on his desk with hands clasped at times, and at others poising his head with his fingers', according to the *Derby Mercury*, Alf stated that Winnie had first mentioned that her mother needed poison on New Year's Day. Alf said his wife had told him it was for 'a guard dog at an internment camp', but that it was Winnie who had 'practically suggested the experiment with curare'. Alf stated he had told Winnie to leave the matter with him, as he had poisoned what he estimated to be around 2,000 mad, sick or old dogs before. He said that he had never before used curare to kill dogs, but that he would be interested to see its effects.

Alf explained that, due to the nature of his work, he was at present exempt from military service, but that he had travelled to Derby just prior to the arrests, en route to Liverpool where he hoped to get a job as a dispenser on a liner. For this reason he had obtained a passport. He had used code in his letter so that his intentions should not be known.

According to Alf, he had first obtained the curare during his apprenticeship, from a friend in Birmingham, and had used it only during classes. Alf claimed that he had not taken the tubes of curare to the college until 1 January, and that he had done so for the use of the students, thus contradicting Maud

Nash's testimony that she had seen the curare two weeks earlier. As he had packed up the tubes to be sent to Derby, he had told his students that the poison was to be used on a dog. Alf told the court that the poisons he had sent would be quite unsuitable for murder because the strychnine would be too bitter and easily detected by any intended victim, and the amount of curare was insufficient to kill anything bigger than the dog for which it was intended. He also pointed out that there was a mistake in the directions: curare would not be effective in 20 seconds, but in 20 minutes. The judge then asked Alf why he would suggest using such a slow-acting poison when prussic acid (hydrogen cyanide) would work in seconds. Alf replied that the dog might be in an awkward position, such as on a wall or difficult to get at, in which case the use of a poison dart etc., would be more effective.

Regarding his offer of the provision of microbes ['If you care for microbe can supply'], Alf told the court it had been intended as a 'sarcastic jest' because the poisons he sent were more than adequate.

When questioned on his anti-war stance, Alf stated that his objections were based on religious, not political, grounds. He was against the taking of life and had advised his lab assistant Cook to take a job as a wireless operator to avoid having to do this.

Alf's cross-examination took place the following day. The *Derby Mercury* reported that a dense fog had descended on London and that there had been a 'palpitating wait' while a tardy juror and judge filed into their seats, in case the whole trial should have to be started over once more. It was Saturday and this was presumably the reason for what the *Derby Mercury* described as 'a much larger attendance of the unemployed Bar'. Friends of the accused were in attendance, too. The newspaper also noted that behind the dock sat a 'compact body of sympathisers with conscientious objectors'.

The Attorney-General began by asking Alf Mason to confirm that he had made some study of criminology, which he did. Sir

Frederick Smith then asked Alf whether he considered himself a 'criminologist'. Alf declined to call himself this: 'That is a matter of opinion.' The prosecutor then put it to Alf that 'half a grain of strychnine has proved fatal to a human being'. Alf said that he had 'not come across such an instance'. He did, however, agree that 'smaller doses than half a grain have given rise to very grave symptoms in human beings'.

Sir Frederick then launched full-flow into his questioning: 'Surely your study of criminology must have been very limited if you do not know that strychnine has been used for the purposes of murder? In these courts we know that.' He also expressed surprise when Alf said that he was not aware of his example, the 'Palmer case'. Certainly this case had been well documented. Dr William Palmer, a Rugeley physician, was convicted and hanged in the 1850s after being found guilty of the murder by strychnine poisoning of his friend John Cook. Much of the case's notoriety was earned when it was revealed that several of Palmer's family members, his children, wife and mother-in-law included, as well as some acquaintances, to whom he owed money, had died unexpectedly, often in Palmer's presence or shortly after meeting with him. Alf agreed that, had he been familiar with the details of the case, he might have had a more accurate idea of the amount of strychnine needed to commit murder.

Sir Frederick asked him: 'Do you remember the Neil Cream case where strychnine was given in sweets?' Alf replied that he did not. Despite Smith's assertions that the case was very recent, having concluded only around 1893, Alf remarked that he was 'scarcely born then'. It was perhaps more surprising that Alf had not heard of this case; certainly it had captured the imagination of much of the country at the time and was unlikely to have faded entirely from the national conscience. At its centre was morphine user Thomas Neil Cream, who was also a doctor. Already convicted of a murder in Chicago, Cream was eventually hanged for the murder of four London women. He had befriended them and, feigning concern for their various ailments, had offered them strychnine tablets that he had disguised not, as the Attorney-General had remembered, as sweets but as medicines. The case was particularly notable because at his execution Cream had claimed to be Jack the Ripper.

Alf Mason might have claimed to have no knowledge of these cases but it was likely that some, if not all, the jurymen knew about them, and by mentioning them at all the Attorney-General had neatly managed to remind the jurors of occasions on which trained medical men, as Alf Mason was, had become killers. 'Is it news to you,' Sir Frederick continued, 'that in many other cases of murder, the crime has been committed by administering strychnine in cocoas, chocolate and sugar-ice, and powdered on bread?' Alf replied: 'I should not have thought it possible.'

The affable Alf, however, was no match for the wiles of the Attorney-General, who then asked him about the instructions he had written for the use of the poison, in particular the phrase 'powder A on meat is OK, or spread on bread'. Alf denied that he had written the words 'spread on bread' and, after some persistent questioning by the prosecutor, agreed that they must therefore have been added in to Booth's copy. 'I sent this poison for the purpose of destroying a dog,' Alf reminded the court.

> Sir Frederick: 'It is suggested by me that the whole story about a dog is, from beginning to end, a lie. Do you understand that?'
> Alf: 'Yes, I understand it.'
> Sir Frederick: 'That being so, supposing these words "or spread on bread" were in your original directions, it would suggest strongly, would it not, that the poison was intended for a human being?'
> Alf: 'Possibly.'
> Sir Frederick: 'Is there any doubt about it?'

Alf: 'Yes, there is, because other things might be given to a dog.'

Sir Frederick: 'Does that occur to you as a sensible observation?'

Alf: 'Yes.'

Sir Frederick: 'Have you ever heard of strychnine being given to a dog on bread?'

Alf: 'No, not on bread.'

Sir Frederick: 'Of the 2,000 dogs you said yesterday you had dispatched, did you ever approach one with poison spread on bread?'

Alf: 'No, not on bread.'

Sir Frederick: 'Did it ever occur to you to despatch a dog with curare spread on bread?'

Alf: 'No.'

Justice Low: 'Or with curare at all?'

Alf: 'No.'

There followed a discussion on the potency of the various forms of poison that Alf had sent to Derby. Tube A, Alf agreed, contained enough strychnine to kill three or four people, but he doubted whether the contents of tube B, another form of strychnine, could be relied upon.

Alf was next questioned about his role in helping to harbour his fugitive brother-in-law. Alf stated that, as far as he was concerned, his brother-in-law was on indefinite furlough from the army, so he had not knowingly harboured him. He knew nothing of his status as a fugitive, or of Alice Wheeldon's arrangements for his escape, even though the plans appeared to involve the chemist's escape too. Alf finished his evidence by stating that he had been travelling to Derby only on business, not in a bid to escape conscription. He also said that he knew no details about the dog in Derby, only that there was one that needed disposing of, and that he did not realise it was illegal to kill dogs. He was, the *Derby Mercury* reported, entirely 'opposed to illegality'. After that, the Wheeldons and Masons had no more to say.

Dr Bernard Spilsbury returned briefly to the stand. He told the court that strychnine had been a cause of death in a number of homicides and accidental deaths and that it could be administered in a variety of ways, including being spread upon bread and butter. He also stated that half a grain of strychnine might be fatal; three-quarters of a grain would certainly prove so.

Herbert Booth returned, too, and testified that, contrary to Alf Mason's claims, he had added nothing to the instructions for using the poisons. What he had written was precisely what Alice Wheeldon had read out to him.

The case for the defence was closed.

Chapter 9

Distracted by Discussion

All his witnesses having appeared before the court, Saiyid Riza stood to address the jury. According to the *Derby Mercury*: 'He spoke rapidly and with great volubility. Sometimes his voice rose till the court rang with his eloquence.' Riza's oration was, on occasions, dramatic as he outlined his fears for his adopted country. At other times it was sympathetic to the Wheeldons' cause. But all too often he tended to ramble, becoming mired in minutiae and distracted by discussion.

Riza began with an attempt to appeal to the social conscience of the individual jurors. He reminded them that they should draw no distinction between the defendants and their supposed victim; each should be dealt with equally fairly. They should 'forget the distinguished position of Mr Lloyd George, the hero of the nation and of the larger part of the world, and deal justice to humbler folk'.

Riza declared that much of the weight of evidence against his clients was based on the words and actions of a man who had not even stood before the court to face examination. The prosecution was, he said, 'scandalous, vile and vindictive'. It was not only dangerous to the accused, but to the whole country. Riza claimed that this was the first trial in English

108

legal history to rely on the evidence of a secret government agent, one so secret that he had not even been called to give evidence in person. What had been the difficulty in producing Gordon before the court? He was the key witness, after all, and 'the man who, in effect, started the plot, and the man who lured the prisoners on; and then, when he had got them well into the net, handed the case over to Comrade Bert'.

In other words, should the jury choose to believe that the defendants were guilty of a plot, then they could surely see that the plot was entirely the construct of Alex Gordon, and that he had acted as an agent provocateur. Riza worried that the pursuit of this case might soon mean that any unassuming individual in the country could find himself or herself subject to criminal investigation on the whim of a single agent. According to the *Derby Daily Telegraph*, Riza told the jury that he hoped it did not mean 'that men and women had to answer to anything that a secret agent chose to enter in his note-book'. He went on:

> I challenge the prosecution to produce Gordon. I demand that the prosecution shall produce him, so that he may be subjected to cross-examination. It is only in those parts of the world where secret agents are introduced that the most atrocious crimes are committed. I say that Gordon ought to be produced in the interest of public safety. If this method of the prosecution goes unchallenged, it augurs ill for England.

Riza revealed that his associates had made every attempt to locate the mysterious Gordon: 'The solicitor in this case has left no stone unturned to find Gordon, and has failed.' It was a clear implication that the authorities had gone to great lengths to keep the agent secreted away. Just to what lengths would become clear only months later.

Without Gordon as a witness, Riza suggested, the trial could not be relied upon. If the court could not be sure of the truth, then any verdict it might produce was random. 'These ladies are charged with a vile and heinous crime and if, in the absence of Gordon, you still wish to try them the proper course would be trial by ordeal.'

Justice Low was taken aback by this suggestion, forcing Riza to repeat what he had said. Even then the judge did not seem to catch the defence counsel's point, remarking 'But trial by ordeal has been abolished. We cannot do it, and what is the use of submitting that suggestion to the jury? No, you cannot submit it to them.' But Riza was determined: 'I submit that in this particular case it would be the safest method.'

> Justice Low: 'Do you suggest that these ladies should walk over hot ploughshares?'
> Riza: 'I do, my Lord, in order to prove their innocence.'
> Justice Low: 'Then they cannot do it.'

This exchange prompted much laughter in court and the judge instructed Riza: 'If you have anything serious to suggest, put it.'

Riza returned to his work, pointing out that the foul language in the letters was not, by itself, evidence of 'a vindictive mind'. He commended his clients' 'engaging frankness' about their beliefs, and said it was proof of their 'natural truthfulness'. He called upon the jury to forget the 'unfortunate language', and, as he claimed the right to use what language he liked, that the accused were entitled to do the same. After all, he told the jury, a leading actress had used the word 'bloody' in a recent play. (There had been a furore when the character Eliza Dolittle in Shaw's *Pygmalion* had uttered it.) And the phrase 'ought to be shot' was merely a colloquialism. Phrases such as this were often used jokingly among friends, and as a turn of phrase during a political crisis. It did not mean that each time a person uttered such a phrase, they actually intended to shoot someone.

The prosecution, Riza argued, had entirely failed to show how the supposed murder might take place. Their evidence was 'inconsistent and inconclusive'. The supposed plot to kill the Prime Minister at Walton Heath was so preposterous, Booth could only have made it up.

Riza then moved on to consider the element of conspiracy. Hettie Wheeldon, he argued, had a busy life. She had a full-time job at the school, a 'young man', and took on extra volunteer work for her political organisations. She simply did not have time to conspire with her mother. It was also clear from the evidence, Riza noted, that Hettie, being more worldly than her mother, had immediately suspected Gordon of being a spy and had communicated these suspicions to her. The jury should also remember, Riza told them, that this was a court of law, not one of politics, and while Hettie did want to bring political change to her country, she wanted to do so by organising the people, not by assassinating the Prime Minister.

It was a point which he laboured at length. Riza's explanation of Hettie's innocence was apparently so long-winded that Justice Low reminded him that there was little point in repetition, and agreed to instruct the jury that there had been no evidence to prove that Hettie had even seen the contents of the parcel.

Neither, Riza told the jury, was there any evidence to suggest that Winnie was, as the *Derby Mercury* had suggested, 'mixed up in a conspiracy'. As for Alf Mason, Riza argued that it was quite impossible that a man of such clear intelligence would make a point of showing phials of poison to his class assistants if he intended to use them for nefarious purposes. There was absolutely no evidence that the poisons he had sent from Southampton to Derby were intended for use on human beings. As for the prosecution's assertion that the Wheeldons had made up the story of the dog, Riza pointed out that this was not a recent addition; Alf and Winnie had written about a dog in their correspondence. For the prosecution's version of events to be true, the jury would have to believe that this

Southampton chemist kept quantities of deadly poison on hand 'ready to offer them to anyone whomsoever wanted to take human life'.

Concluding his summing up, Riza told the court that the case against his clients ought not to have taken so long, since it was a very simple one. It was perfectly evident that they were innocent.

According to the *Derby Mercury*, Riza's 'unusual' speech, which lasted 3 hours and 40 minutes, had 'at first amazed, then rather bored' those in attendance. There had been considerable dismay when it had transpired that, even after a lunch break, Riza intended to continue. The *Mercury* described the rather theatrical response of the prosecution team to Riza's verbose statement:

> Mr Attorney sought rest in slumber, Mr Hugo Young devoted himself to cultivating a resemblance to the late Sir Henry Hawkins – he too slept, but with one eye open, Sir Archibald swapped jokes and smiles with a colleague, and one other member of the Bar seemed to be sucking his thumb.

The jurors too, it seemed, were beginning to tire of the process and it was unclear to observers whether Riza's words were having the desired impact: 'The Wheeldons and Masons followed the counsel with smiles, but the jury looked stolidly to their front, and one or two of the most industrious occasionally made notes, but their faces displayed no emotion.'

Riza did make quite an impact on the watching press corps, although perhaps more for his foreign peculiarities than the force of his argument. The *Derby Mercury*'s correspondent noted that although he 'was not always coherent . . . one felt a kind of sporting sympathy for him – as Englishmen are bound to feel for a little chap who is fighting big ones'. Indeed, Riza approached the fight 'undaunted', assisted only by a single solicitor, and up against the might of the Attorney-General, two King's Counsels and a junior, 'to say nothing of perhaps a dozen expert advisors'. But there was little hope: 'It was like a cockleboat defending a derelict against Dreadnoughts.'

The *Derby Daily Telegraph* expressed less sympathy, concentrating primarily on Riza's foreignness. He used, it claimed, 'a foreign language, and his English has a curious Welsh intonation'. Their correspondent did not think much of his legal skills either, informing readers: 'He would have done better to concentrate on the two or three outstanding weaknesses of the Crown case, instead of lavishing an Oriental subtlety on giving an innocent turn to the peculiarities of the Wheeldon style.'

Predictably, perhaps, Sir Frederick Smith's closing remarks were largely a straightforward reiteration of the evidence put before the court. According to the *Derby Mercury*, he spoke 'very quietly, almost in silken tones' and 'argued that agreement and participation constituted conspiracy'. He said that there was not a man on the jury who, knowing what they did of the Wheeldons, would not say that the use of Gordon was justifiable; that if the case was not proved without Gordon, the jury were entitled to acquit the accused; but that nothing had been elicited to prove Booth unworthy of their belief; and that his story was supported by statements of the accused, as for instance in regard to the microbe incident, which Mrs Wheeldon denied, but which Mason admitted was a joke. (In fact Alice had denied personally offering Gordon and Booth a microbe, not that Alf had done so in the instructions.)

Sir Frederick claimed that 'Mason was as bad as anyone else in the family in this business'; that Winnie and Hettie, despite 'the appearance of the innocence of their youths still preserved, showed the degeneracy of their surroundings'. He described as a 'desperate invention' the suggestion that the poison had been acquired for dogs.

In the second hour of his speech Sir Frederick ran through the pertinent facts of the case that, the *Derby Mercury* decided, 'need not be recorded again'. As it transpired, neither Saiyid

Riza nor Sir Frederick Smith needed to reiterate the facts as they saw them, for the esteemed Justice Low was more than happy to advance much of the argument for them. In what the *Derby Mercury* described as 'the most powerful and striking oratorical display', the judge spoke for 1 hour and 25 minutes. The *Derby Daily Telegraph* described it as 'short, masterly and scrupulously balanced . . . the most important thing in the long day of legal argument'. The *Mercury* outlined his points:

> It was a lamentable case, lamentable to see a whole family in the dock; it was sad to see women, apparently of education, using language which would be foul in the mouths of the lowest women. Two of the accused were teachers of the young; their habitual use of bad language made one hesitate in thinking whether education was the blessing we had all hoped.

However, Justice Low did remind the jurors that they could not convict the women on grounds of foul language, only for 'conspiracy to murder' and that 'if the jury were not convinced of that, they had no right to convict'. He outlined the need for proof of conspiracy: 'they must be judged by their acts'.

As to the alleged intended murder weapon, 'the use of poison to kill was just as dastardly, whether it was employed against the Prime Minister or the humblest subject of the Crown'.

Although Riza had been quite right in pointing out Gordon's absence, which Justice Low called 'the singular feature of the case', the jury had still to consider the evidence that was put before them. The judge defended the use of secret agents, noting, according to the *Derby Daily Telegraph*, 'Without them it would be impossible to detect crimes of this kind.' He warned the jury to consider carefully Booth's evidence. If they did not believe him, then the case 'to a large extent fails'; if, however, 'he was telling he truth, then Mrs Wheeldon was steeped in crime'. The judge continued: 'The manner in which poison was obtained was highly furtive.' He asked them to consider 'the explanation about the poison being needed to kill a dog'.

There were questions that needed answering regarding discrepancies in the defendants' statements: if, as Alf had alleged, Will Wheeldon was not the fugitive his mother had claimed, why then did Alf think he needed to be concealed?

Justice Low had shown considerable contempt for the defendants throughout the trial, but at this point he did make clear an unexpected sympathy for Hettie, directing the jury that, if they thought she might not 'be at one with her mother', then they could acquit her. The judge thought that Hettie seemed 'self-willed, not likely to lend herself to an enterprise concocted by others'.

It could be argued that since there was no evidence that Hettie had either seen the poison, or discussed it, it was impossible to prove that she knew anything of any plot, whether to kill a guard dog or a prime minister. Justice Low, it seemed, agreed. He suggested that the existence of the poison had been deliberately kept from her by her mother, and he told the jury that they must then consider why this was so. They must decide if it might be something more serious than the killing of a dog to necessitate such secrecy. He believed that if the jurors chose to acquit Hettie, it 'made the dog story additionally ridiculous'. He believed that, as Hettie was the local organiser of the CO movement, it was 'improbable' that a plan to free such men from captivity would be kept from her. In other words, if Hettie was innocent, it was all the more likely that the rest of her family were guilty.

Justice Low then discussed the contents of the letters and the supposed 'divergences' in the defendants' stories about the microbes. He ended his summing up by reminding the jury that, in addition to the conspiracy charges, Alice was also charged with soliciting both Gordon and Booth to murder.

And then it was done. All the evidence was heard, the

arguments presented, accusations made and innocence protested. All that remained was for a conclusion to be drawn. The twelve men entrusted with that duty retired from the court. As they left, Hettie and Alice betrayed no emotion. Alf and Winnie exchanged smiles and conversed with their counsel. For a brief while, they all left the dock.

At twenty minutes to eight, after less than half-an-hour of deliberation, the jury returned to the court. The defendants were recalled and stood, each with a warder behind them, to hear their fates. There was complete silence as the foreman stood and delivered the verdicts:

> Alice Wheeldon: guilty on both counts.
> Hettie Wheeldon: not guilty on all counts.
> Winnie Mason: guilty of conspiracy.
> Alfred Mason: guilty of conspiracy.

Chapter 10

Even Keyholes Have Ears

The pale figure of Hettie Wheeldon stood motionless in the dock. Astonished at the verdict – the convictions of her mother, her sister and her brother-in-law, but her own acquittal – she did not move until Justice Low ordered her immediate discharge. A wardress motioned for Hettie to follow her and she looked from right to left at the family that surrounded her and then left the dock without comment.

Mr Justice Low then spoke to Alice Wheeldon, who had stood stony-faced since the jury foreman had delivered his verdict:

> You have been convicted upon evidence which could only have brought the jury to one conclusion – namely that you conspired and solicited and proposed the crime of murder, and murder by poison. Poisoning is one of the gravest crimes that can be committed. The law limits to a certain period the extent of the sentence that can be passed upon you. I can imagine no worse case than yours, and I have no alternative but to send you to penal servitude for ten years.

117

Alice parted her tight lips to mutter only a quiet 'Thank you' to the judge, and without further reaction also left the dock, accompanied by a wardress.

To Alfred Mason the judge spoke deliberately. He had chosen to take into consideration the jury's advice to afford the Masons leniency 'in consideration of their youth'. Justice Low told Alf: 'But for the recommendation of the jury, I should have passed the same sentence on you. You will go to penal servitude for seven years.' Alf surprised those in court by leaving the dock with 'almost a jaunty step' and a fixed smile on his face. The *Derby Mercury* suggested: 'Perhaps he was thinking that, after all, he had escaped military service.'

Winnie, now alone in the dock, betrayed no discernible emotion as Justice Low addressed her:

> With regard to you, Winnie Mason, you also without question were a party to this nefarious scheme. I take into account your bringing up, and I feel that your position is largely due to the bad and wicked influence of your mother. The jury have taken the view that some leniency should be shown to you, and I shall pass upon you the sentence of five years' penal servitude.

With that, Winnie too was taken from the court.

There was to be one last act in the 'Great Poison Plot Trial', as many newspapers had come to call it. Mrs Emmeline Pankhurst was at last permitted to defend the honour of the WSPU. She told the assembled court: 'We declare that there is no life more valuable to the nation than that of Mr Lloyd George. We would endanger our own lives rather than his should suffer.'

As matters finally came to a close, the court erupted into excited chatter. Amid the finely attired society ladies, the court reporters and the curious legal professionals stood Edith Marshall, Alice's niece by marriage and a reluctant witness for the prosecution. Although supported as she was by the

Wheeldons' allies, the *Derby Mercury* noted she 'was much affected by the result'.

While the mood of those within the court was reasonably measured, the same could not be said of the journalists and editors whose newspapers spread the news across the Western world. As far as the press was concerned it was now open season on the prisoners and a seemingly ever-increasing hysteria accompanied each new report of the verdict, although the *Daily Mail* chose to stick with the brief facts, leading with: 'Guilty of Plot to Kill Lloyd George . . . Mason, Wife and Mrs Wheeldon sentenced to five to ten years' penal servitude . . . Harriet Wheeldon Acquitted.'

The international press, however, saw little need to prevent the facts of the case from getting in the way of a good story. North American newspapers in particular seemed to have witnessed entirely different trials as they added 'facts' here, and reinterpreted the evidence there. The *Washington Post*, for example, wrote about the 'subtle poison plot nipped by the secret service. Remarkable details of the plan to kill the English Premier with Chemicals, Microbes or Snakes'; the *Sandusky Star* referred repeatedly to 'Inspector Gordon of Scotland Yard'; while the *Kansas City Star* implied that there was a list of assassination targets and that the various 'bright ideas' for murdering Lloyd George included 'sticking a poison pin in his hat and allowing him to scratch his scalp with it', and even 'harking back to the days of Cleopatra, one project was to destroy him with a serpent'. Alice Wheeldon, the paper explained, 'had the skin of a baby adder stuffed and made into a bracelet, a poison bracelet that would end the life of whoever wore it'.

In Britain, and in Derbyshire in particular, the aftermath of the trial led to intermittent hysteria of a different kind. Just as after the Breadsall fire innocent women gathered in a church-yard were supposed by panicked onlookers to be arsonist Suffragettes, there was widespread concern and suspicion that schools were filled with an army of 'Socialist' teachers who were bent on indoctrinating the nation's young against King and Country.

Within the Socialist movement itself the mood was more one of consternation at the verdicts, and at the manner of the Old Bailey trial. Protests had been brewing for some days. On 6 March 1917, the day the trial began, the Leicester 2nd branch of the Amalgamated Society of Engineers had drafted a letter to the Home Secretary informing him of a resolution they had passed at their most recent branch meeting. It was entered into Home Office records on 13 March, three days after the convictions. The resolution read as follows: 'We demand that the Police Spies, on whose evidence the Wheeldon family is being tried, be put in the Witness Box, believing that in the event of this being done fresh evidence will be forthcoming which will put a different complexion on the case.'

Another Leicester organisation, this time the Leicester & District Trades Council, met on 8 March, and again two days later, to discuss the Wheeldon case. They too had written to the Home Secretary on the Wheeldons' behalf. This resolution, received by the Home Office on 10 March, copied virtually word for word the resolution of the first. And on the 10th yet another identical resolution was delivered in a letter written by David Ramsay, secretary of the Leicester Engineering (and Rank and File) Amalgamation Committee. That the Leicester Socialists should be so well organised, and so confident that had Alex Gordon appeared as a witness then Alice, Winnie and Alf might not now be in prison, was intriguing but not a coincidence. In February Alderman George Banton of Leicester had been a speaker at the Derby ILP. According to a report filed by a government infiltrator, after being told about the case he 'advised that all Pacifists should try to secure a just hearing for the Wheeldons, without doing anything that would compromise Pacifist principles'. He had called the secret agents 'dirty skunks and moral leopards'. It would later emerge that Gordon had Leicester connections.

For Alice and Winnie, who had been taken immediately to

Holloway prison, and Alf, who was now incarcerated at Wandsworth, lodging appeals was of primary importance. Like the trial itself, the resolution of the appeals was swift. On 7 April, less than six weeks after their convictions, all three family members were informed that their leaves to appeal their convictions and sentences had been refused. There is scant record of this process. There was little need – the appeals were refused outright in a matter of days.

In the meantime, her name officially cleared, Hettie had returned to Derby, to 278 Normanton Road, less than 200 yards from Alice's now deserted shop. But the authorities, it seemed, were not finished with her. On 16 March Sir Charles Matthews of the office of the Director of Public Prosecutions wrote to the Home Office regarding Hettie's case: 'I have the honour to forward the undermentioned documents for consideration as to whether the case of Harriett Ann Wheeldon, the Defendant who was acquitted, is one which calls for any action under No. 14 B of the Defence of the Realm Act.' This regulation allowed the authorities to intern anyone suspected of being of 'hostile origin or association'. Enclosed with the letter were a transcript of Hettie's evidence, a photograph of two letters she had written while on remand, a copy of a letter sent to her while in prison, and one of Colonel Labouchere's reports.

One of Hettie's letters was to her brother Will, who was now interned in Hylton Castle Camp near Sunderland. She writes nothing damning to her 'Dear Will', only general chat about mutual friends, her mother's mood and the expected date of the trial. The second letter was to Willie Paul's wife back in Derby: 'We are all well, in good spirits, and wish you were all here with us to get a long-earned rest, and a peep into the prison system, of which more when I see you.' But she admits these words are 'inanities' because, with her letters being censored, she is unable to say more. There are, however, some allusions to her revolutionary beliefs:

Cheer up, we must expect things like this in our fight against the System . . . eyes and intellects are opening, in spite of the 'war'. Men are beginning to realise their real enemies, and for so much we should be devoutly thankful. Keep the flag flying and adjust tactics accordingly. It's our move next.

The third letter had caused quite a stir, although it had never reached Hettie. Sir Basil Thomson, the head of Scotland Yard's Special Branch and Deputy Commissioner of the Metropolitan Police, had passed it to Sir Charles Matthews. Written by one 'Alexander Green' of Glasgow, the letter had been sent to the Pear Tree Road shop. It began: 'I am extremely sorry that you have not been successful in your plot to kill Lloyd George and the Right Honourable Arthur Henderson . . . and I hope with all my heart that the next plot will be successful.' The rest of the letter consisted of a string of expletives aimed at the King and a declaration that 'I am proud that I am a Pro-German'. Unsurprisingly, perhaps, attempts by Special Branch men to track down Alexander Green had proved fruitless.

The minutes of a meeting held at the Home Office on 19 March 1917 reveal that officials were well aware there was little chance of rearresting Hettie. They read: 'It would require a strong case on the merits to justify interning, under Regulation 14 B, a woman who has just been acquitted; but in this instance . . . do not think that the question arises.'

Correspondence to a dear brother, political statements to an old acquaintance, and a crank letter from someone who in all likelihood was unstable were simply not damning enough to allow the authorities to hold Hettie.

'Hostile', it seemed, was deemed only to refer to enemies of the country and in Hettie's case, while the evidence did show her to be 'an associate of conscientious objectors and other disaffected persons . . . there is no trace of association with any German, Austrian, Bulgarian or Turk'. After a week's deliberation Home Secretary Viscount Cave, via his under-secretary Sir Edward Troup, informed Sir Charles that detaining Hettie in this way would not be possible.

Meanwhile, Alice, Winnie and Alf waited desperately for news from the outside world. As prisoners, their access to newspapers was controlled and it was unlikely that they would be permitted to read their favourite radical journals while detained at His Majesty's Pleasure. Letters, of course, both in and out of the prisons, were intercepted and censored. But from those that did make it to friends and family outside, we can learn a good deal about conditions within the institutions and the family's reactions to their incarceration.

Several of these letters came to light when the *Derby Evening Telegraph* published extracts from letters from Hettie and Alice to Lydia Robinson. Lydia and her daughter Dolly ran a health-food shop at 117 Normanton Road, Derby. The letters, which had been discovered by Mrs Robinson's grand-daughter Fay Kidger among her grandmother's belongings, are intimate and largely upbeat in tone. While still on remand, Alice had seemed in high spirits. She joked with 'Aunty Lid', thanking her for a box of cakes and promising: 'I'll do as much for you when you are in clink.' Both women wrote about the 'small holding', or allotment they kept, advising that there should be some celery ready for harvest, and reminiscing about 'tattering'.

Alice revealed that she had advised her eldest daughter Nellie not to come to visit her. Hettie, too, discouraged visits while on remand and explained: 'Not that we don't want you, but in the first place it isn't worth the expense and in the second it is not safe as New Scotland Yard secret agents . . . are on the prowl, and even walls and keyholes have ears.'

They maintained their political fervour, Alice signing off: 'Thine in the courage of internationalism, the world is my country, is it thine? God save the people'; while Hettie quoted part of a poem by Robert Browning: 'We fall to rise, are baffled to fight better, sleep to wake.'

The close relationship between the two families is apparent;

Alice had told Nellie to make regular visits to the Robinsons, and some weeks after her conviction she thanked Lydia for 'taking care of my girls'.

Although they were not permitted to describe the prison in much detail, Hettie estimated that there were around 900 women in Holloway, while Alice contented herself with a detailed description of her bed:

> It is the nobbiest arrangement I have ever seen . . . spring mattress in the framework, on two upright legs fastened into the floor. One side is fastened like a post and rail and the two other legs on the other side will turn down when the bed is put straight out for use. So you see when it is not in use it rears up against the wall making the place tidy and sanitary.

Matters in the outside world were never far from Hettie's thoughts. She complained that 'the guns from Woolwich [more than 10 miles away] keep booming', reminding her of the war in progress. She noted that conditions in the prison are not so bad compared with working-class houses: 'If the poor, honest, excluded submerged tenth only knew that in prison there is rest, quiet, comfort and good food, I don't think they would toil and sweat, curse life and live in a slum as they do.'

Within weeks, however, Hettie was becoming concerned for her mother's welfare. Shortly before the trial, in a letter to her brother Will, Hettie speaks of the 'marked effect' imprisonment is having on Alice: ' . . . but then what does it matter to anyone? You can die fifty times for all anyone cares.'

Both Winnie and Alice were to spend much of their sentences at Aylesbury prison and we can learn much about daily life there in 1917 from Anne Marreco's biography of another infamous Aylesbury inmate, Constance Markiewicz. An aristocrat – she was a countess – Markiewicz was a Suffragette and Irish nationalist who served time in Aylesbury for her prominent role in the Easter Rising of 1916. Marreco records that there was little privacy for the inmates. In the centre of each cell door was a carved and painted eye; a constant reminder that on the other side was a sliding disc which could be lifted by prison guards so that they could observe the prisoners without themselves being seen.

The women were woken at 6.30am and after washing and dressing were given breakfast in their cells. They received 6 ounces of bread and a pint of tea, which was usually cold. At 10am those women sentenced to hard labour were given a ration of 2 ounces of cheese and another small piece of bread. Lunch, eaten at 12 noon, usually consisted of 2 ounces of meat, 2 ounces of cabbage, a potato, a thick flour gravy and another 6 ounces of bread. On Thursdays a hard cold suet pudding was served, and on Fridays it was boiled fish. At 4.30pm a pint of cocoa or tea and another 6 ounces of bread were provided as supper.

From her arrival at Aylesbury, Alice began a campaign of non-cooperation and awkwardness, punctuated with intermittent hunger strikes. Prison officers and fellow inmates saw nothing of the caring soul so doted upon by her family, nor the unflappable witness who had given evidence in her own defence just weeks earlier. If the countless reports made by the prison staff are accurate, she had quickly become an angry, moody, sometimes threatening and frightening woman, perhaps on the edge of mental breakdown. It is impossible to say whether the degeneration in Alice's behaviour was entirely deliberate, or whether the ravages of the trial, imprisonment and malnutrition played their part. Whatever the contributing factors, Alice's time at the prison was to turn into a disturbing series of events.

Soon after her arrival at Aylesbury in April 1917, she was transferred to the infirmary, where she spent several weeks. Dr M.E. Staley, the deputy governess and medical officer at the prison, described how Alice 'was from the beginning rude and offensive to the nurses and officers. We gave her plenty of time to settle down; but in May I reported her to the Governor [Dr

S.L. Fox] for her bad behaviour . . . and described the woman as a "wild beast" owing to her continued evil words and conduct.'

In June prison medics reported that Alice 'remained in quite good health and put on weight – 5lbs', and she was moved into the ordinary cells. But Alice's behaviour, merely obstinate at first, seems to have become ever more militant as the weeks wore on. She was required to do prison work, but, according to her daughters, became angry at being transferred from the garden to the laundry, where she did needlework. G. Daley, one of the prison matrons, noted that while working at this 'she appeared sullen always and rarely spoke to me'. The matron stated that Alice would laugh to herself when the governor or doctor visited the workroom. One prisoner named Elwood complained to Daley that Alice had sworn and cursed at the officers, and told the other prisoners 'they were fools not to strike out against the rules'.

At Aylesbury prisoners were subjected to regular random searches of their person. One officer reported that during such a search a number of letters had been found on Alice, as well as a piece of tissue paper on which she had written the dates of letters and visits she had received. Alice told the officer they were not important, and that she could keep them. She then pulled off her calico shift, removed her flannel vest and handed it to the officer saying: 'Do you want this? You may as well have it – there is a limit to a woman's degradation.' Alice had then sat down and begun to cry. When the officer tried to comfort her, explaining that she was only doing her duty, Alice replied: 'Then it is a great pity young women could not find some better duty to do.' Another officer, during another search in which some of her clothing was removed, noted Alice's defiance: 'Whatever you take off me will remain off until I am in a box, you dirty, lazy, low-down crowd, you can't get an honest living or you would not be here.'

Prison staff reported that Alice's tactics were often juvenile and were usually unsophisticated. J. Jones stated that 'when I attended Dr Staley to see the complaining sick in the work-room, Wheeldon asked for a jersey and Dr Staley told her she could have one . . . as soon as Doctor's back was turned she looked round to other prisoners, laughed, and put thumbs up. I reported the matter to Dr Staley as soon as she came out.'

On several occasions Alice was accused of threatening violence. Once she complained about a cold in her back and was advised to see the doctor or governor. Alice had refused, saying: 'Where there is incompetence, there is always tyranny.' When a matron had told her to calm down, she was heard to threaten to 'pitch her over the blasted banister'. Prison officers reported that, as the year wore on, they began to receive complaints about Alice from other prisoners. One reported that Alice said something 'to Prisoner Flick': 'I asked Flick what was the matter. She replied: "Nothing miss, only Wheeldon says all the bloody officers want burying. I am afraid of that woman."' Several other prisoners apparently reported that 'old Wheeldon' was 'always trying to agitate the women against the officers'.

However ill she may have become, it seems Alice was in no mood to abandon her political interests, perhaps even pressurising fellow inmates to help her. Dr Staley wrote:

> Brooke, the prisoner whom she had suborned to take out cryptic messages for her to the WSPU, told me much of her methods, and other prisoners told me that she threatened them so that truly they went in fear of her. She used to curse them under her breath if they would not do her bidding. One wealthy prisoner asked me for a tonic as she was so sleepless and shaken by a 'worry' burden pressed [*sic*] to relieve her mind of it to the chaplain . . . she told me (in strict confidence) that she was terrified of Wheeldon, who cursed them and seemed to 'have a devil'. She thought she might get her into trouble or even 'do her in' for not obeying her.

If Alice did bully her fellow inmates, then she was a terrifying figure indeed, for Aylesbury was home to some of the country's most hardened female convicts. Constance Markiewicz had herself been part of James Connolly's Citizen Army during the Dublin Easter Rising, and was second-in-command at St Stephen's Green where the street-fighting rebels held out against the British Army for six days. Another notorious prisoner was May Duignan, known as Chicago May, an Irish-born American prostitute and con-artist, who had been imprisoned in Aylesbury for the attempted murder of her boyfriend. Markiewicz recalled meeting Alice in a corridor of the prison. The pair had exchanged a few words, Alice declaring her innocence, before warders hurried the pair apart.

But it was Alice's intermittent refusal of food that caused the prison authorities most concern. On 23 November 1917 she refused food once more, threatened to go on a 24-hour hunger strike and was returned to the infirmary. J. Jones reported that when Alice was admitted to hospital: 'She told me that she would not eat a crumb all the time she was in hospital, and that she would throw the bread out of the window as soon as my back was turned.'

Nurse Ethel Yarwood believed that Alice's behaviour was entirely calculated: 'One could tell by her manner that she was just taking stock of things and biding her time.' She also described a typical day during Alice's hunger strikes:

> She refused all food . . . but drank plenty of water. Hot milk was taken to her at 4am the next morning but it was untouched at 6.30am when I unlocked her. She refused breakfast at 7am. When Dr Baker [an occasional visitor to the prison] visited her she asked what she was in hospital for. Dr Baker told her he understood she was run down and needed rest and quiet. 'Quiet do you call it,' she said, 'with [all the] moans and groans downstairs?' Another prisoner was being treated nearby for nasty burns.

It seemed Alice knew what effect her hunger strikes were having. She told Dr Baker: 'If you feed me you will kill me and I shall have obtained my object. The inquest afterwards will do for you more good than I ever shall.'

An officer named E.A. Jeffs had told Alice that she must eat something for fear of worrying Winnie. She reported Alice's reply: 'Damn the daughter, I won't touch it, I've put down the hammer. I told you what would happen if I was degraded again. What I say I mean, you ought to know that by this time.'

On 7 December, with her condition somewhat stabilised, Alice was returned to the ordinary cells and four days later received a visit from Hettie and Nellie. On her way to the visiting box, Alice told matron E.W. Harp that she 'wished a bomb would drop on this bloody hole and blow it up'. Alice was overheard telling her daughters: 'You could not beat a woman for petty tyranny and systematic cruelty; men were bad enough but for grinding down and brutality you must look at a place ruled by women.' Apparently delighting in the news that other COs had joined her son at Durham, she said it was 'time for a revolution in England'.

One of the officers heard Alice referring to Dr Staley as 'an Indian fakir'. Dr Staley was very concerned by Alice's behaviour, having been subjected to numerous insults and curses. Alice 'called me a Lazy Devil, consigned me to Hell . . . boasting that we should all suffer a terrible retribution . . . we were the enemies of mankind and must be done away with'. The doctor also reported that Alice's manner had caused tension with other prisoners. One had told her: 'You must feel yourself very good to curse everyone as you do and threaten murder like this,' only to be told by Alice: 'It is not merely murder, but a judgement coming upon these bloody beasts.'

'Of course,' noted Dr Staley, 'I only quote this as told me by the prisoners who reported it and it may not be true.' But the doctor went on: 'She is a dangerous woman I should say and she and her daughter, W. Mason, seem to have many friends and followers who admire and uphold them, judging by the letters that come from them to the prisoners about the "pack-up" [revolution] to which they are all looking forward.'

That Alice found the energy to cause such disruption is testimony to her obstinacy, for she was continuing her hunger strikes with added determination and on 21 December began another. The prison governor decided it was now time to attempt to force-feed her uncooperative inmate. T. Mann, one of the matrons, recorded:

> On 23 December at 11.40am I was present and assisted when Wheeldon was fed with a spoon. Prisoner was violent, breaking a feeding cup by knocking it out of Dr Staley's hand. She was also very abusive, calling the governor, who was present, a hypocrite and flaming vampire, telling us to get away, or she would tear our flaming eyes out, exclaiming: 'This is a so-called Christian country,' using abusive language all the time.

Dr Staley told her: 'You can be too determined sometimes,' to which Alice replied: 'You may, but I am not.' Staley also recorded that Alice 'is obstinate and quite impervious to reason'. And Alice was certainly determined. Although she complained about the cold, she refused to drink tea. The matrons gave her 'extra blankets and a hot bottle'.

Papers held at the Home Office reveal that up to Christmas Eve the use of a more violent form of force-feeding – with a feeding tube – had been under consideration. Dr Dyer, a visiting medic, who had been instructed to 'thoroughly examine' Alice, reported that, given her existing ill health (she had arteriosclerosis, gout and a weak heart), it would prove 'very dangerous to feed her by tube, especially as she is senile for her years and being powerfully built would . . . offer a good deal of resistance'. Dr Dyer, it seems, had noticed a mental frailty in Alice not accounted for by her prison guardians.

Although the method of force-feeding they had attempted

was not as dangerous as others, it still carried great risks. A Prison Commission report for the Secretary for Scotland in 1909 had pronounced: 'For prisoners who offer resistance it is a method attended with considerable risk of injury . . . considerable damage might be done to the prisoner's mouth.' It was highly unpleasant too, with the mouthpiece of the cup forcibly pushed between the prisoner's teeth, or between the gaps if they had any teeth missing, and the contents poured into the mouth. There had been a considerable public outcry when it had emerged that the practice, normally reserved for 'lunatics', had been used on female prisoners in British jails.

Dr Staley reported that it would be quite impossible to force-feed Alice, even with a feeding cup, without the presence of two doctors. She noted: 'Removal to a prison elsewhere with two medical officers is urgently advised.'

Just days after Alice's conviction, the Home Secretary had received a letter from Mrs Mary Bullar, cautioning:

> Mrs Wheeldon and both the Masons left the Dock after their sentence smiling [newspaper reports contradict this]. Obviously they intend to punctuate their sentence by going on hunger strike and so to bring the law into contempt. Could you not bring in a Bill at once simply to say that forcible feeding was to be abandoned – that all prisoners alike would be given their meals regularly and that it rested with them to eat them or not as they chose – it was the forcible feeding that made the outcry so there could hardly be one at giving it up!

But simply allowing Alice to starve herself to death was not an option the government could easily stomach. On Christmas Eve a number of Home Office staff met to discuss Alice. Dr Dyer had reported that he saw little point in moving her back to Holloway, where there were two doctors, since this would not induce her to eat. The possibility of releasing Alice under the

'Cat and Mouse Act' – allowing her to go home to regain her health and then rearresting her once she was fit enough to continue her prison sentence – was considered. But there were fears that, once free, 'if she renewed her attempt on the life of the PM it would be impossible to justify having released her'. The officials also knew that 'release [under the Act] in time becomes permanent and, even if the intervals of release are made as short as possible, she could find an opportunity for attacking him, or could invite some other reckless person to do it'.

A proposal was made that Alice should, as Mrs Bullar had suggested, be told she would not be forcibly fed, and that she could not be released, and warned that she must accept the consequences of her actions: 'The latter course ought not to be taken unless we are prepared to adhere to it to the end' (which would doubtless result in Alice's death in prison). It was, indeed, 'a critical decision'. But releasing Alice carried its own risks.

If the Home Office were to release a woman sentenced to ten years in prison for conspiracy to murder, then any criminal 'however bad may find it worthwhile to make the same attempt . . . if the Secretary of State decides to release her, we must keep her till the last moment that is safe and must make every effort to get her back again after a short interval. But it will be an unpleasant business.' But with Alice now accepting only hot water, and given her decreasing mental stability and frail health, the Home Office decided to transfer her from Aylesbury to Holloway. Dr Dyer was instructed to arrange this.

When Dr Staley informed Alice she was being moved, she told the doctor that she would not cooperate. She refused to dress in prison clothes and instead was given several blankets to keep her warm en route, which she 'held together' as she 'walked quietly downstairs to the taxi'. One of the matrons who escorted Alice, E.A. Jeffs, reported: 'As the motor-car started, she said: "I wish the Germans would come and blow the bloody place up brick by brick and all of you bloody swines with it."' Although Alice refused to take any milk on the journey, Jeffs reported that 'when near Watford [she did] take half an ounce of stimulant'.

Once Alice had been moved to Holloway, Sir Edward Troup, the permanent under-secretary to the Home Office, took a personal interest in her condition, receiving daily, sometimes twice-daily, reports of her progress. On 26 December an official of the Prison Commission reported:

> I have been in telephone communication with Holloway . . . the prisoner's pulse was a bit rapid, but this would be accounted for by the journey. Otherwise she seems well and there is no sign of collapse. She appears to be determined in her attitude not to take food, as she remarked . . . that she was going out either in a coffin or in some other way. I told [the doctor] to put tempting food in her cell and use all persuasion possible and he promised to do this.

The following day it appeared that Alice's condition had deteriorated sufficiently for the Home Office to begin considering further measures: 'Her pulse is quicker than it was yesterday . . . there is no need for any action yet, but . . . release might have to be considered by Saturday, and discretion to release over the weekend, if found necessary should be considered . . . the woman says she is going to die on Saturday but [the doctor] does not think the case so bad as that.'

As word of Alice's failing health reached her family and friends, her sister, Ellen Land, sent a telegram to the prison: 'Can I see Alice Wheeldon who I believe is in a critical condition?' Dr R.W. Paton, the governor of Holloway, recommended this be allowed as 'it might have a good result'.

On the 27th Dr Wilfrid Sass, the deputy medical officer at Holloway, reported that Alice's condition was rapidly declining: 'Her pulse is becoming rather more rapid . . . of poor volume and rather collapsing . . . the heart sounds are rapid . . . at the apex of the heart . . . she complains of some pain.' It was decided to ask Alice's family to intervene once more and a telegram was sent to Hettie in Derby. It read:

> Secretary of State desires to inform you that your mother Alice Wheeldon has been refusing to take food for several days and is thereby endangering her life. She is now in Holloway prison. You will be allowed to visit her at any time . . . if you are unable to bear the expense of the journey to London apply to Chief Constable of Derby.

At the same time the Chief Constable was informed that, should Hettie ask for funds, he should 'please advance money which will be refunded'. On the evening of 27 December Hettie and Nellie made the first of several visits to their mother. According to the governor's letter to the Prison Commissioners, the matron observed the meeting: 'The language used throughout was appalling . . . the name of Jesus Christ used in blasphemy. She [Alice] also spoke of vengeance – getting blood for blood.'

Alice was heard using the word 'sod', and referred to the Aylesbury governor, Dr Fox, as a 'foxy bitch' and as a woman who would 'shit on you and rub it in'. She also 'expressed a wish that all the Borstal girls might be struck stiff as they are a bad lot'.

On the same day the Prison Commission contacted Dr Fox at Aylesbury, where Winnie now resided alone. A note from Alice to her daughter was enclosed, along with instructions that Winnie should be allowed to write to her mother in Holloway, although any reply had to be sent via the Prison Commission. Winnie had been told that her mother had been moved and that she was again on hunger strike. She believed that her mother was protesting about having been moved from Aylesbury and that, unless she had a good reason to continue her hunger strike, Alice would soon eat again. The

Prison Commission hoped a letter from Winnie would encourage her.

Alice had a restless night, much of it spent lying awake crying. According to Home Office officials, a visit from her daughters the next morning 'had not been of any use'. In fact Alice was heard to refuse her daughters' pleas to take food, and declared that she was 'going to die and that there would be a great row and a revolution as the result'.

Despairing, Hettie and Nellie went immediately to the Home Office for a meeting with Sir Edward Troup and other officials who had been following their mother's condition. The report of the meeting reveals Hettie's belief that Alice was protesting at her treatment at Aylesbury 'which she described as a long course of petty annoyances culminating in the final degradation of being stripped naked'. This differed from accounts by prison staff and it is likely that the truth lay somewhere between the two versions. The officials asked Hettie for specific instances of mistreatment, and were surprised that she could only 'mention changes of work . . . and arrangements at exercise which appear to have been intended to prevent the undesirable association of Mrs Wheeldon and her daughter Winifred [sic] Mason'.

The women were advised they should again meet their mother and attempt to persuade her to end her protest, but Hettie told Sir Edward that she doubted this would work. 'Her mother had reached such a point that she did not care to live with the ten years' sentence in front of her. She did not think that she would take food even if she were allowed out.'

Hettie also told Sir Edward that Alice 'was in so apathetic a condition she did not even want to see her and objected to her coming'. She did not think her mother would live very much longer, although Dr Paton and Dr Dyer disagreed.

Hettie asked Sir Edward whether her mother's sentence might be reduced 'say, after the war'. But she was told that since her mother's offence was 'against the ordinary law of the land' and because her appeal had failed, no such promise could be made, although it 'must not be excluded'. All agreed that if Alice were released only temporarily, she would still refuse food. The only thing that might cause her to end her strike was the promise of a substantial reduction in her sentence. The report of the meeting ended with one conclusion: 'I do not think there is any chance now that the mother will give in.'

On 30 December Winnie Mason wrote to Hettie in response to a letter describing the meetings. It seems that Winnie had little idea of the severity of her mother's illness. Her letter makes for poignant reading:

> I've re-read and re-read your letter to try to grasp it but my brain simply reels at – it's too awful . . . When I was told she'd gone to London ('It's a very large city,' as I was informed when I asked: 'Where in London?') I thought they'd taken her to Broadmoor and I prayed that she might die and be spared that last agony . . . When the next day I was told she was in Holloway in the hospital and was alright, I can't describe.

Winnie was in despair:

> What I am to say to our sweet mam? Even though I realise it's more merciful for her to pass over than to continue the mental anguish she's been enduring, I can't resign myself to it – when you think of her beautiful life of sacrifice and devotion to us all – in fact to everyone who knew her, and then think of what she has undergone this last year – it makes you wonder if there isn't a great fiend overruling everything, doesn't it?

An even more distressing letter, from Winnie to Alice, revealed much about her own anguish during their imprisonment. It began:

> My own sweetest Mamsie . . . when I think of all the
> opportunities I've had of giving you a kiss or saying some-
> thing to you and I've restrained myself rather than
> imperil our chance of association . . . and then this to
> happen – oh it's too awful. I could never forgive myself . . .
> you do know why I've kept myself away, don't you? You
> don't think it was because I didn't love you, do you? I'd
> give the world to have these last 9 months back again!

The authorities had intentionally kept the women apart as
much as possible, and it was revealed by Dr Fox that Alice had
at one point resorted to persuading one of the other prisoners
to pass notes to Winnie.

The letter continues:

> Are you suffering much, Mamsie – fancy them moving
> you without me seeing you . . . I knew you were ill and
> suspected what was happening though I wasn't told it
> of course, the suspense and my imagination made me
> feel bad and I suppose you've been worrying because
> you've thought I was worrying.

It is clear from her letter that Winnie found it very difficult to
ask her mother to yield on a matter of principle. Indeed, Hettie
had told Dr Fox that she would write to her mother only if it
were not conditional on her advising her to give up her hunger
strike. Winnie wrote:

> Mam darling, don't let any thought of that [Winnie's
> fears] hinder you in anything you want to do – I know
> you've restrained yourself more times than enough for
> my sake already, and although I can't bear the thought
> of losing you – as you of course must know that's what
> it will end in if you go on – I'm not going to ask you to
> do anything you've made it a point of conscience with
> yourself not to do.

And yet, as a loving daughter, Winnie could not help but plead with her mother not to allow herself to die: 'Oh Mam, please don't die – that's all that matters . . . you've been a real brick and a darling since you were born . . . oh Mam, you mustn't die – you were always a fighter but this fight isn't worth your death.'

Winnie reveals their separation had been unbearable:

> Can't you feel me near you, Mam? I shall be with you darling Mam – don't worry any more about us – try and get better yourself but if – I can't write it hardly – it should be this is going to be the end, Mamsie, you'll wait for us all won't you? . . . Oh Mam, for one kiss from you! Oh do get better please do, live for us all again.

Realising she might never see her mother again, Winnie added one last goodbye: 'Should I never have another chance Mamsie mine this kiss will tell you how your own Babs [as the youngest child it was a nickname of Winnie's] Win loves you and loved you to the last in spite of everything and everybody.' At the end of her letter Winnie placed a large inky 'X'.

The sentimental picture of Alice's character painted by her youngest child was in stark contrast to that produced by Dr Fox. Realising that the Home Office was considering the release of her former inmate, the governor wrote to officials cautioning against such a decision:

> I consider the prisoner a deep, dangerous, malicious scheming woman of particularly evil character . . . she has a violent and uncontrollable temper . . . she has threatened to put in motion such forces as will wreak so terrible a vengeance on me that all will hear of it . . . On Dec 22 . . . she had every appearance of wishing to attack me with personal violence, but owing to the presence of several officers she refrained.

To back up her allegations, Dr Fox enclosed witness accounts from many members of her staff about Alice's behaviour. But the accounts would make no difference. A higher power was about to step in and determine Alice's fate.

On 29 December the Home Office had received a phone call from David Lloyd George's private secretary to say that the Prime Minister had 'received several applications on behalf of Mrs Wheeldon, and that he thought on no account should she be allowed to die in prison'. The Home Secretary had also received a telegram from the liberal evangelical Russell Maltby. It was short and to the point: 'Hearing Mrs Wheeldon seriously ill. I beg you release her and avoid tragic end to what was possibly cruel blunder.'

And there it was: there were a great many people who were unsure of the validity of the case in the first place. To allow the death, in custody, of a woman whose very conviction was still hotly debated was quite unthinkable.

Sir Ernley Blackwell, a legal assistant under-secretary to the Home Office, met with Lloyd George in person to discuss the Home Secretary's reluctance to release Alice. The Prime Minister urged that Alice could be released on licence on the grounds of her severe ill health. According to the official papers: 'He evidently felt that, from the point of view of the government, and in view especially of the fact that he was the person whom she conspired to murder, it was very undesirable that she should die in prison.'

It was a fait accompli. The Prime Minister himself had intervened. There was simply no way to hold Alice Wheeldon in prison any longer. Notice was sent to Holloway that the licence for her release was being prepared, and in mid-afternoon Dr Paton informed her that her ordeal would soon be over. According to reports Alice initially refused food, perhaps fearing this to be a ploy to get her to eat, but the governor eventually persuaded her to take her first meal in nine days: 'Some Bovril and gravy.' When Dr Fox informed Alice that she was being released at the personal intervention of the Prime

Minister, she replied: 'It was very magnanimous of him . . . he has proven himself to be a man.'

With Alice agreeing to take a little food, her health showed immediate improvement and by the next morning she was fit enough to be released. Before she was permitted to leave, Dr Paton read out to Alice the terms of her licence. Then, with Hettie and Nellie beside her, she left Holloway in a taxi bound for St Pancras station where she would at last catch a train home to Derby. According to Reuben Farrow, a man the trial had revealed her to despise, and one of only a few souls who bothered to witness her arrival at Derby's Midland station, Alice was bewildered and weak and had to be helped along the platform.

On 31 December Dr Paton wrote to the Prison Commission enclosing a neatly handwritten letter from Hettie Wheeldon. It was remarkable primarily for its civility and matter-of-fact tone. It read:

> Dear Sir,
>
> My mother wishes me to tell you that she had a comfortable journey. We managed to secure a warm compartment in a dining car to ourselves. She says she is suffering no ill-effects from the change of residence. Many thanks for your courtesy and considerate treatment.
>
> With best wishes for the New Year.
> I remain,
> Yours sincerely
> Hettie Wheeldon

Now came the sticky problem of informing the public that a woman who had been declared a virtual traitor only a few months earlier had already been awarded her freedom. For several days the newspapers had been carrying stories of Alice's failing health, preparing the public for her imminent death. Instead they were to learn that she had been freed.

From his weekend home at Burnham-on-Sea in Somerset the Home Secretary sent a telegram to Sir Edward Troup informing him that the public should be told the precise details of Alice's release. And so it was that the Home Office press bureau issued a statement to newspaper editors across the country, informing them of the momentous decision:

> The Home Secretary has decided to advise the release upon License of Alice Wheeldon, who was convicted in February last at the Central Criminal Court of conspiracy to murder the Prime Minister and sentenced to ten years' penal servitude. This decision has been taken at Mr Lloyd George's express request.

With her business closed, and many of her former friends and neighbours having turned their backs on her, Alice Wheeldon had only the support of her immediate family and a few faithful friends and allies; life would never again be easy.

After Alice's release, attention turned towards the plight of Winnie and Alf Mason. In 1918 a campaign group produced a leaflet to this end. It was entitled: 'Victims of Alec [*sic*] Gordon, the Agent Provocateur.' Eventually public pressure produced results and on 26 January 1919 the pair were also released on licence, as newspapers reported, 'at the request of Premier Lloyd George'. Like Alice, the Masons would also find life on the outside much changed.

Chapter 11

Agent Provocateur

Among Socialist and pacifist movements at least, the imprisonment of the Wheeldons and the Masons had served only to heighten the sense of disquiet they had felt at the non-appearance of Alex Gordon during the trial. From the moment the story broke, these groups had expressed serious concerns at the use of secret agents to gather evidence about their organisations. According to once-secret reports filed in the Home Office archives, one agent, known only as 'No. 6', who was still active in Derby on 17 February 1917, noted: 'What these good people are worrying about is the presence in their midst of government spies.' No. 6 was probably Lieutenant Frederick Wisotzky De Valda, a man with his own intriguing history. Born Fritz Wisotzky in France around 1884, the son of a Prussian-born but naturalised French businessman named Augustus, his early life was spent in Hartington Street, Derby, ironically just doors away from the CO hideaway owned by Miss Marsden. According to his colourful autobiography, he travelled the seas from the age of 16, teaching in Australia and witnessing the great Jamaican earthquake of 1907; the details of his life read like a John Buchan novel, causing one sceptical associate to comment that he must have been 'about 150 years old or capable of being in two places at once'.

Perhaps because of the uncertainty about who was genuine and who was a government agent, many groups were quick to distance themselves from the Wheeldon family. According to De Valda/No. 6: 'All the pacifists have been greatly perturbed by the disclosures in the Wheeldon case . . . they are almost tumbling over each other to explain that the Wheeldons are not members of their respective organisations.'

Several of the groups had already worked out the identity of at least one agent of the Ministry of Munitions. According to No. 6: 'Major Lee is mentioned as he has been in Derby on several occasions in connection with these investigations . . . these "facts" are stated by the official of the Derby ILP who appears to be following what he calls "clues".'

It was not long before protests against the use of secret agents became a national issue. In March Ramsay MacDonald, MP for Leicester and the man who had resigned as leader of the Independent Labour Party in 1914 in protest at the war, spoke in Parliament about the dangers of using 'agents provocateurs [who] make their money out of the manufacture of crime', citing specifically the case of Alex Gordon. Another Labour MP, William Crawford Anderson, the member for Sheffield Attercliffe, himself a trades union organiser, tried to get the Labour Party to investigate Gordon. He also tried and failed to persuade Sheffield shop steward Walter Hill to give evidence about alleged encounters with Gordon. A wealthy anarchist, J.M. Davison, even offered a reward for the discovery of Gordon. But the agent was nowhere to be found.

In Major William Melville Lee's report and 'short resume of the Wheeldon story', which is dated 5 December and so was presumably written almost a year after the event, Lee states that Gordon had gone to Derby 'on general instructions to get in touch with revolutionaries and people likely to commit sabotage'. The town's munitions production and radical Socialist connections made it an area of interest for the security services. Lee stated that Gordon had arrived in Derby on Boxing Day of 1916, although agent No. 6's report suggested that he may have been there as early as 8 December. He had gone to the Socialists' Hall at the ILP centre in Derby. A man named Dupuy, probably William, an engineer of 62 Abington Street, had taken him to the Clarion Club in the Wardwick. There he had been introduced to various NCF members, who had directed him to Alice's shop. Lee described Alice as an 'extreme anarchist' with an 'invalid husband who spends most of his time at the Clarion Club'.

One of the problems with sending in outsiders to gather information was that they could report only what they could actually observe, or gather in hearsay; they had no background intelligence with which to gain perspective. It was some time before Winnie Mason's existence even became clear to the agents, and at first they did not know she was married, only that she had at some time embarked on what was termed a 'trial marriage'. The local police, on the other hand, provided more detailed information. It was they, for example, who reported William Wheeldon senior's drinking habits.

For all the apparent cloak-and-dagger workings of the agency (which gave its agents code names: Booth was 'No. 4', Gordon 'No. 5', etc.) the whole system of having spies infiltrating rebel organisations was largely unregulated. Although men like De Valda came from well-off backgrounds and were experienced men of the world, the same could not be said of every operative.

Having been sent to a particular town, agents acted mostly of their own volition, following leads as they chose and coming into contact with their superiors only when they had something significant to report. But the most troubling aspect of this method of information-gathering was that many of the so-called 'agents' were nothing of the sort. They were in fact little more than paid informants, with no espionage training; worse, they were often paid only on results. The better the information supplied, the more the informer was rewarded. Far from being motivated by serving their country, the informants' interests were purely financial and they knew that the more salacious the information gathered, the better their earnings. Consequently they were often tempted to exaggerate or even invent information to ensure a healthy wage. It was a risky and entirely unsatisfactory way of acquiring intelligence.

Major Lee's first report of December 1916 stated that he did not entirely believe Gordon's claims about the Wheeldon family: 'As will be seen . . . the whole story is nothing beyond the recital of certain incriminating statements alleged to have been made by a woman and her daughters who are probably all but crazy.'

But Lee had a strong dislike for Socialists, and in particular for Willie Paul. When Gordon claimed that he thought 'the poison plot was discussed with Willie Paul', Lee was 'not inclined to believe this', but it gave him precisely what he had been looking for: an indication that people associated with identified troublemakers were trying to bring down the government. Lee was certain that there was in Britain a giant conspiracy of radicals, well organised and ready to act at any moment. It was true there were various individuals and groups who were determined to stop the war, and others who wanted to bring Socialism and Communism to power by any means possible, but this idea of a centrally administered, single organisation of like-minded individuals was far from the truth. The fact that Alex Gordon was able to continue to gather intelligence on various pacifist and Socialist organisations without being detected, even after the Wheeldon story broke, is proof of this. But this was not surprising. Major Lee's imaginary behemoth did not really exist. It was not an organisation, but a loosely associated, many-headed movement. Communication between the disparate groups was neither speedy nor complete.

Despite his doubts about Gordon's accuracy, Major Lee reported the Wheeldons to be 'criminals in intention, if not in deed. Not quite sane, but possessed of considerable cunning and just the sort of people to tempt a weak-minded man to commit sabotage, arson or even murder.' But Alex Gordon, in the pay of the security services, was nothing of the sort, and Lee's superiors, and others concerned with intelligence-gathering and law enforcement, were even less convinced than Lee of their agent's reliability.

Gordon's true identity remained shrouded in mystery. One might be tempted to believe that he was so vital to the war effort, his role within the Ministry of Munitions so important, that the government simply dared not allow his identity to be uncovered. However, it is clear from Home Office papers that Gordon was at the very foot of the intelligence services' ladder. Even before he came into their employ he operated under a number of aliases: Herbert Vincent and Albert Richard are supposed to be among them; and he openly used both Francis Vivian and William Rickard. His evidence, as the very first person to uncover the poison plot, would surely have proved powerfully persuasive in court. And yet Attorney-General F.E. Smith chose not to call him. In the months and years after the trial several descriptions of Gordon's appearance, demeanour and behaviour emerged, shedding some light on that decision. In his somewhat fanciful account of the trial, written some years later, Smith, by then Earl Birkenhead, stated that Gordon had ceded control of the case to Booth because he was 'beyond his depth' and that Booth, who was 'well known in the Temple . . . made a more suitable desperado than Gordon'. More probably he made a more suitable witness.

Concerns about Gordon's reliability were raised by Sir Basil Thomson, head of Special Branch and Assistant Chief Constable of the Metropolitan Police, whose permission to intercept and open the Wheeldons' and Masons' post had been sought by the Ministry of Munitions. According to the Metropolitan Police's history of Special Branch: 'Sir Basil Thomson was deeply concerned about spies and subversives.' Certainly he would have been keen to halt any perceived threat to the country. And yet in Thomson's own book *The*

Story of Scotland Yard he reveals his misgivings about the case, writing that a 'military officer [Colonel Labouchere], who had been appointed intelligence officer to the Ministry of Munitions . . . proceeded to unfold a fantastic story'. In this story 'a family in one of the Midlands towns' was apparently plotting to assassinate Lloyd George. The plan involved a 'stooping man' who would hide behind a bush on the Prime Minister's favourite golf course and shoot a poison 'blow-dart' at him as he passed. This would eventually send him into 'a sleep from which there would be no waking'.

Thomson wanted to meet the mysterious Gordon before acting further, but his suspicions were aroused when Labouchere told him that Gordon had shown 'great unwilling-ness to come', particularly when Thomson's name had been mentioned. He had also made it a condition 'that his name should not be disclosed'. Thomson revealed: 'That set me thinking; either the agent was a person with a criminal history, or he had invented the whole story to get money and credit from his employer.' To try to establish the validity of Gordon's claims, Thomson obtained the warrant to stop and examine the Wheeldons' post. The contents of the first intercepted letter, in which Alice had referred to Lloyd George 'in oppro-brious terms', made Thomson think there might be some truth in Gordon's report. Yet still he had 'an uneasy feeling that he himself might have acted as what the French call an agent provocateur – an inciting agent – by putting the idea into the woman's head, or, if the idea was already there, by offering to act as the dart-thrower'.

Thomson informed Labouchere that his agent must be brought to Scotland Yard, whether he 'liked it or not'. Labouchere tried to avoid this, telling Thomson that Gordon was of a sensitive nature, and a poet 'with all the nervous shrinking from publicity that is supposed to go with poetic inspiration'. Thomson was undeterred: 'I said that I was sorry to have to outrage his poetic feelings, but in a case of such gravity I must insist.'

Before Gordon could be brought to London, however, the investigation moved on apace with the arrival of the poisons in Derby. Once the package was safely in the hands of their agents, and out of the reach of the supposed plotters, the authorities were in no immediate hurry to act. According to Thomson, Labouchere then brought Gordon to see him and the Director of Public Prosecutions. Thomson instructed the superintendents of the Fingerprint Department and CID to 'wait outside the conference room and cast a searching eye over the agent when he passed them on his way upstairs'.

Thomson noted: 'Then there walked into the room a thin, cunning-looking man of about 30, with long, greasy, black hair. My superintendent sat up and stiffened like a setter at the scent of game. He called in the fingerprint expert and whispered to him; the expert hurried off.' Gordon, it seemed, was concerned at this development, exhibiting 'extreme nervousness when he saw the manoeuvre, but he replied to all our questions readily enough'.

Then an 'unseen hand' on the other side of the door gave the superintendent two cards 'each bearing a photograph . . . both photographs were speaking portraits of the long-haired poet, but the names on each differed, and neither of them was Gordon'. Alex Gordon, whoever he was, had come to the notice of the police on more than one occasion. But with the discovery of the poison, and despite his own grave concerns: 'We had to use the man; there was no alternative. We could only observe whether he would come with credit through his cross-examination.'

However, for F.E. Smith there was an alternative: he simply refused to call Gordon as a witness. Smith later asserted that Gordon 'was not a material witness, as he dropped out at the very beginning'. This was certainly not the case but rumours that Gordon was eccentric, or even mentally unbalanced, that he had met Walter Hill in Sheffield and told him of plans to kidnap Lloyd George, and offered bombs and poison to various individuals, among them Arthur McManus, simply would not go away. It mattered little that the rumours could not be substantiated. Had they been voiced by a defence witness, or during any cross-examination of Gordon, they would surely have dangled a doubt before the jury. It was a risk the prosecution could ill afford to take and Gordon was secreted away until after the trial.

Indeed, nothing more was heard of Gordon for almost three years. Then, in early December 1919, he unexpectedly presented himself at the offices of the *Derby Daily Express* offering to sell information 'to anyone about anything'. According to reports he had in his possession a revolver and one bullet and had said that he intended to settle a score. He was removed from the premises by the local constabulary, but later turned up at another Derby newspaper where he was greeted more warmly and given money with which to buy a meal. The first paper reported that the Police Court Mission offered to pay his fare to Leicester, and Gordon left the town, presumably for good.

Some three weeks later, on 27 December, Gordon's somewhat pretentious and moody photograph appeared on the front page of the *Daily Herald* under the headline 'Alex Gordon'. For those who had avidly followed the case it was the first opportunity to either hear from, or see, the famous absent witness. Inside was an interview given by Gordon, now claiming to be Francis Vivian, just returned from exile. The front page featured an article by the journalist 'C.B.H.', revealing 'How I Got Mystery Witness of Wheeldon Case to Talk'. Given that Gordon had seemed keen enough to talk to the press in Derby, it had probably been less of a challenge than the *Herald*'s reporter implied.

Inside, the headline promised much: 'How I became Alex Gordon'. And the interview, if taken at face value, offers an interesting insight into the enlistment of intelligence agents, their methods and activities. The interview, conducted in five hours over two days in a 'certain provincial town', reveals Gordon to be an odd, somewhat eccentric individual with a well-honed and theatrical narration style. He seemed consumed by paranoia, and wandered restlessly around the room. He was, the journalist revealed, initially affable, although non-committal. He appeared to be 'making a great effort to control his condition of haunting anxiety and nervous dread'. He moved around the room with a 'catlike and soft' tread. He seemed suspicious and questioned the reporter at length before satisfying himself that this was the man from the newspaper to which he had been writing. He was 'rambling over numerous subjects' and 'presented the attitude of an innocent sufferer, haunted and hunted by physical fear of – he could scarcely say what'. Gordon was jumpy too: 'The scarcest sound outside the door made him start violently, and then he would draw the window curtain back and peer out into the darkened street.'

Throughout the interview Gordon clutched a book containing newspaper cuttings and photographs. He claimed to have been working as a journalist for the *Leicester Mail*. At the end of 1916 he had been writing a series of articles exposing people posing as spiritualist mediums. He told the interviewer that he had been approached by a man [probably this was Booth, although in the article he was known only as 'X'] who told him he represented a publishing firm which wanted someone to obtain information comparing 'non-militant Socialism and extremist action which would be likely to help the Germans'.

'X' claimed that his 'guv'nor [in reality Major Lee] . . . is a crank on Socialism' and had been so impressed by Gordon's articles that he believed he was the man for the job. Gordon had accepted the job 'on condition that names were not to be mentioned'. He seemed not to have been surprised at the offer and stated: 'The proposition was merely a common incident in a journalist's career.' A few days later 'X' visited Gordon again and told him that the firm had 'made very careful and searching inquiries about me and were quite satisfied that I was capable of getting the copy for the book'.

Gordon was told that 'X' had tried to get him £3 per week, but his guv'nor had limited payment to £2 10*s* with bonuses 'if the copy was coming in well'. 'X' told Gordon that the guv'nor wanted 'fairly exciting copy, and in fact the more exciting the copy, the better the guv'nor would be pleased'. Clearly, Booth was no stranger to the tried and tested methods of the secret services. However, Gordon was told he 'must get facts'.

Gordon told the interviewer that he had once been a member of 'a Socialist group'. He had, however, only peripheral knowledge of such groups and referred to the members as 'Our Socialist friends'. He revealed that he thought it had been his own idea to take on the Alex Gordon persona.

'X' had taken Gordon to London's East End where the pair had spent several hours trying to find the Great Tongue Yard, off Whitechapel, where the IWW had its headquarters. Gordon said 'X' had eventually had to go into a police station to check a map of the local area. When they finally arrived he told Gordon to go inside and 'to get at the truth', assuring him 'this is the only way to get it'. Gordon accepted 'X's assurances that: 'There is nothing particularly wrong about it [spying] and no names will be published and no harm done that way. You will be setting forth a list of facts. You will be able to state the case as to militancy and the attitude of any people who may be there towards the war.'

Even the casual observer might think that Gordon had been extraordinarily naïve, or perhaps simply conceited, in not questioning why he in particular had been selected for such research. In the interview he claimed he was 'very simple'. He said that 'X' had taken away his army medical discharge papers and registration card. He claimed that the financial rewards promised were so great, he dare not question the terms: 'I thought it was a decent job, and there was more money in it than I had been getting. I had a lot of worry and misery and I did not want to lose this chance.' Gordon revealed he felt threatened, too: 'And there was always this menace held over me. If I appeared to hesitate about anything "X" would say: "You are no good, I can get another journalist to do the job".'

At times during the interview, Gordon had seemed to drift off into his own thoughts and, while he did not ramble, it was hard for the journalist to keep him talking about the more pertinent elements of his story. Gordon said that inside the IWW headquarters he had found the place almost deserted, except for a few people: 'no Englishmen . . . there were a couple of Americans'. He noted that he had seen pamphlets in a foreign language: 'I believe it was Hebrew.' He had been given several leaflets and had kept them, thinking it might be useful 'if I could get it translated'. One man had offered him a new pair of boots to replace the old ones he wore. But when he met with 'X' later that day, he had been surprised to be asked to draw a plan of the building's interior. He told 'X' he had no gift for drawing and instead had described the interior at some length, and taken 'X' to the building to see the entrances. A few days later the reason for this interest was to become clear. 'Much to my surprise,' Gordon claimed, 'X' had come to him and told him that the building he had been in, and described in such detail, had been raided by the police. Interestingly, during the trial Booth said he had told Alice that he had been present in the building during the police raid. The journalist asked Gordon if he had wondered whether there had been a link between his recce and the raid. Gordon replied: 'If I ever put anything of that sort forward, it was always put on one side.'

Next, Gordon claimed, he had been sent to a Communist club he thought might have been on Fitzroy Square near Regent's Park; in fact it was in Charlotte Street. This time, because he had 'half-a-crown' on him, 'X' refused to give him any more money, telling him to 'go there and see how you are received if you are hard up'. Again the premises were raided shortly after Gordon's visit.

Gordon explained: 'You see, I was hanging on to this blessed job, and hoping it would come all right. I was thinking of my wife all the time and wondering what "X" was going to do with my army cards, and what would happen if the police pulled me up.' But 'X', Booth, or whoever the mystery handler was, promised that 'the guv'nor had plenty of influence and if I were arrested [he] would be able to put things right'. Even this guarantee, it seems, did not alert Gordon to the true nature of his employers. He continued to work for 'X' for 'five or six months' without incident. He was then sent to Manchester. By this time, he said, he was coming under greater pressure to uncover something more sensational. When Gordon could find nothing to report in Manchester, he 'got into a bit of a stew because I said there was nothing doing and nothing to report . . . well, what was it that happened? Some little tramway strikes in Salford.'

'X', it seemed, was less than impressed. '[He] knocked off writing to me for days. I wrote several times to him but he did not answer. I said to myself: "I have trusted this man and he has deserted me now and I have no money to send my wife." I wrote again to him and said I did not think the tramway strike would make good copy.' Of course 'good copy' was not what 'X' or his guv'nor were looking for. Any hint of industrial action, such as a 'little tramway strike' was their target.

Gordon did not reveal to his interviewer just when he realised he had become a government informant, or how this had happened, only that: 'By the time I was told that I was – that the government had got me – I suggest that it had . . . and nobody knows better than me . . . it had a hold over me and a very strong one too, that made it absolutely impossible for me to come straight out into the limelight, I could not do it. It was impossible.'

The interviewer asked Gordon the nature of the 'hold' and he replied: 'Economically I mean. I never had any money properly. I did on one or two occasions get a £2 bonus, but they were isolated instances. I never got the 50s in one heap. I always had to sub to get money to go on with. I could not do anything else, I was always in a state of chronic hard-upness.'

Gordon refused to speak directly about the Wheeldon case, or even about his time in Derby. Nor did he offer any information about where he was secreted during the period between the arrests and the end of the trial, a period when the defence team, and numerous others, had been searching for him. He did reveal that on 5 April 1917 he was sent to South Africa 'on the *Athenia*'. In fact the ship was the RMS *Athenic*, part of the White Star Line. Passenger records confirm the date and destination, specifically Cape Town. There, on the passenger manifest, are the details not of 'Francis Vivian' but of one Mr W. Rickard, a 29-year-old 'gentleman' of no specific occupation. His unnamed wife accompanied him.

It is by no means certain that Gordon's birth name was William Rickard, and searches of national archives, birth records and census returns indicate several William Rickards of the appropriate age. But if he was travelling under this name, he must have been issued with a passport confirming this identity. It was at least an official alias.

Gordon said he was instructed that an agent would meet him in Cape Town and give him 'letters of introduction'. Before he left he was awarded £100 and £5 expenses. 'Probably you can guess how soon I got through that,' he complained. To supplement his income, Gordon performed a professional mesmerism act under the rather dramatic name 'Vivid – the Magnetic Man'. He supplied the newspaper with a particularly brooding photograph of himself in his stage costume.

It apparently took some considerable persuasion to get Gordon to sit for another photograph. For a man so reluctant to have his image recorded, Alex Gordon certainly struck quite a memorable pose.

Gordon's interview caused quite a storm. His account was, according to Sylvia Pankhurst, a 'sordid story, and one which the Lloyd George government will doubtless wish to forget'. But they would not be allowed to forget, the Wheeldons' allies saw to that. John S. Clarke, a regular contributor to *The Socialist*, was not about to let matters lie. He wrote an

'Epitaph on Alex Gordon' which the journal's editor, Tom Bell, published, and quoted in his own autobiography.

> Stop! stranger, thou are near the spot
> Marked by this cross metallic,
> Where buried deep doth lie and rot,
> The corpse of filthy Alick.
> And maggot-worms in swarms below,
> Compete with one another,
> In shedding tears of bitter woe,
> To mourn – not eat – a brother.

In February 1921 Herbert Booth sued the *Daily Herald*, its printers and proprietors for an article in which it had compared him to the notorious agent 'Oliver the Spy' who, in 1817, in the employ of the government, had incited a group of discontented radical workers from north Derbyshire and Nottinghamshire to set out for London intent on revolution and the establishment of a US-style federation. Three of the ringleaders had been hanged, drawn and quartered in Derby. In truth, Oliver's role as agent provocateur was curiously akin to that not of Booth but of Gordon. Oliver was never called to give evidence. And while Gordon had been identified as William Rickard, Oliver was later named as William Richard.

According to the *New York Times*, in court Booth admitted working for PMS2, effectively a branch of MI5. He did not mention specifically the Ministry of Munitions. Among other matters, he had been enlisted to 'track down the reasons why a number of shells from certain factories had defective fuses'. He stated that posing as a conscientious objector was his idea and claimed that he had been universally known as 'Brother Bert' or 'Comrade Bert of the Run'. He stated that Alex Gordon was employed by the same department and that the two worked extensively together, which seems to confirm the suggestion that Gordon's 'X' was, in fact, Booth. He testified that revolutionaries always warmly received him, and that at one meeting he had 'the satisfaction of seeing someone else turned out as "Booth the Spy"'. Under cross-examination he admitted sometimes buying alcohol to ingratiate himself with his targets: 'His cue was to pose as an affable, jolly fellow. Beer was a very good weapon for that.' The jurors, three of them women, one of whom 'knitted serenely' throughout, found in his favour and he was awarded £500 damages, although the newspaper lodged an appeal on the grounds that the judge had refused to admit evidence about Gordon.

It was clear from the accounts of both Gordon and Booth that the government had an organised, probably extensive, network of informers and agents actively investigating the enterprises of those groups and individuals who were opposed to the war, whether they fell under the auspices of the Ministry of Munitions or what became MI5. But their accounts, and in particular Gordon's behaviour, call into question even more their methods and motives.

According to No. 6's report in February 1917 many Socialists believed that:

> This Wheeldon case has been deliberately planned for the purpose of discrediting Socialism and the conscientious objectors . . . it is said that Lloyd George, yourself [possibly Major Lee or Colonel Labouchere] and Booth and Gordon had arranged the whole thing and Mrs Wheeldon, being excitable and bitter, [was] just the kind of person you were looking for . . . the view that Gordon suggested the whole thing is, I find, rather general.

However, not all Socialists thought the Wheeldons were entirely blameless. One member of the Clarion Club had told No. 6 that the Wheeldons 'were bloody mugs and fell into the trap'.

Major Lee was certainly not the only establishment figure to fear a Socialist uprising. The belief that Socialist agitators and union activists might bring munitions manufacture to a grinding halt was widespread. The beginnings of what would become the Russian revolution were rumbling away and there was a general mistrust of left-leaning politicians. Persons of interest, such as Willie Paul, were watched with growing concern by the secret service, and it is not surprising that the correspondence of dozens of individuals was routinely searched. Fear of the enemy and of 'un-Britishness', too, played its part in an over-riding atmosphere of fear in which the authorities came to believe that the use of secret agents and informants was their only option.

Chapter 12

Last Farewells

The conditions of Alice Wheeldon's licence imposed strict restrictions on her. Should she venture from her home, she was required to carry her licence with her and 'produce it when called upon to do so by a Magistrate or Police Officer'. Needless to say, she had to avoid participating in any illegal activity and avoid association with 'habitually bad Characters, such as reputed Thieves and Prostitutes'. The authorities need not have worried; the trial and her conviction had earned her so much notoriety that there could scarcely be a soul in her home town who would not know who she was; secret activities would be nigh on impossible. In addition, her physical condition had been so badly affected by her time in prison that she would never know good health again. The second-hand clothes business, too, had been ruined during her time in prison and her infamy had sent all but her closest friends and family running for cover. Alice was ostracised by former neighbours and customers, and not leading 'an idle and dissolute Life without visible means of obtaining an honest livelihood', as her licence required, would require all her ingenuity and effort.

Hettie, too, had lost her income, having been dismissed from her teaching post. She had worked tirelessly for the release of her mother, sister and brother-in-law and had met Sylvia Pankhurst, the Marxist daughter of the WSPU's Emmeline. Hettie had been forced to work on the family's allotment merely to make ends meet. Alice's husband William was working as a shop porter, although he and Alice were no longer living together.

Writing in the *Workers' Dreadnought* in January 1920, Sylvia Pankhurst recalled meeting Alice in Derby after her release. Pankhurst and several of her colleagues had been attending a Labour Party conference in the town, Pankhurst herself as a delegate. During a break in proceedings, Hettie had taken them to the shop on Pear Tree Road. Pankhurst wrote that Alice 'was "mothering" half a dozen other comrades with warm hospitality in a delightful old-fashioned household, where comfort was secured by hard work and thrifty management'. Her shop, it seems, was now closed and Alice 'made the best of the situation by using her shop window for growing tomatoes'.

As financially desperate as she was, and even though she knew she was under the eye of the authorities, Alice was not about to give up her political activities. During 1918 she received regular visits from many of her contacts from the SLP and NCF, including Tom Bell, who recalled those visits in his autobiography. He was often in the company of Arthur McManus, who had become romantically involved with Hettie Wheeldon.

By the end of 1918 Derby was feeling the effects of the advancing 'Spanish' influenza outbreak. Thanks to massive troop and population movements, caused by the war and its aftermath, the virus had spread from one population centre to another very rapidly. It is estimated that between one-third and one-half of the population became ill. It was a virulent, aggressive strain and at least 2 per cent of its victims died. It was as dangerous for young, otherwise healthy, adults as it was for children, the elderly and the sick. Recent studies

suggest that the virus turned the immune system against itself;
the healthier the immune system, the more quickly the victim
succumbed. It proved to be the most devastating outbreak of
disease in recorded history, causing 40 million deaths world-
wide. In one year alone more people died of influenza than in
four years of the Black Death in the fourteenth century. It
claimed more lives even than the First World War itself. In
Derbyshire alone several thousand people perished. Alice,
Winnie, Alf and Hettie all fell ill. Like most of those who died,
Alice, Winnie and Alf developed pneumonia; Winnie and Alf
had been out of prison for less than a month.

On 21 February 1919, just 14 months after her release from
Holloway, Alice Ann Wheeldon died. She was 53. She had
spent her last few months at the family home at 907 London
Road. Her sister Ellen Land, who still lived on Pear Tree Road,
had attended her during her illness and was present at her
bedside as she passed away. It was unlikely to have been a
gentle death – contemporary accounts record many victims
struggling for every last breath. There was no need for a post-
mortem, since the 'flu symptoms were all too familiar to Alice's
physician, Dr Claude Druitt. Around the world newspapers
that had devoted so much space to Alice's sensational trial ran
only a couple of lines about her demise. The Derby papers
were scarcely more generous.

A funeral was arranged for 26 February. The family were
fortunate that they were able to bury their mother so quickly;
in many other areas the number of deaths was so great that
families might have to wait weeks to arrange funerals. On the
afternoon of Alice's funeral, what the *Derby Mercury*
described as 'a small coterie of people' gathered outside her
home. But the family had already arranged for her body to be
removed and the funeral cortège of four coaches left from
'another part of the town'. Reporters observed their arrival at
Nottingham Road, where the town's main public cemetery
sweeps down from the main road, covering several acres.
Among the mourners were Ellen Land with her son William;

Edith and Charles Marshall; Lydia Robinson of the NCF; Arthur McManus; Willie Paul and John S. Clarke; and Arthur Hayward, the conscientious objector whom the Wheeldon letters had described as having narrowly eluded the police at his home. His wife Ada was also there, as was another CO friend, Bert Parker. According to Tom Bell, the Masons 'hovered at death's door for several weeks' and neither they nor Hettie, also ill with influenza, were able to attend.

Young Will Wheeldon was there, however, having been unexpectedly released from Hylton for the occasion. His attendance had been the subject of several telegrams and letters between the Home Office and the governor of Hylton, who had been told that only the Home Secretary could permit his release. Two wreaths bearing the messages 'They knew her best that loved her most, from Her Dear Ones' and 'With Deepest Sympathy,' from the enigmatically signed 'AG, M, T, A and C', were the only adornments. Will's placing of the red flag on his mother's coffin featured prominently in newspaper reports, but it was John S. Clarke's 'sensational' funeral oration that caused the greatest interest.

His disdain for the Christian 'anthropomorphic phantoms of man's imagination', his accusations of 'judicial murder' and his calls for the mourners to 'go back home not with love and sympathy but with intense hatred against what fills the world with warfare, poverty or crime and all such as that' may have stirred those gathered into cries of 'Hear, hear!' but they did not impress the assembled journalists. The *Derby Daily Express* told its readers: 'In his paean of praise of the dead, he sneered at the living.'

There had been no mention at the funeral of Lloyd George, at least not by name. At this the newspaper was outraged. It was, after all, he 'whose wise humanity was such that on learning of the illness of her who would have launched the fatal blow against him gave release for her depressed body to be succoured and her tired spirit to be given rest'.

Their mother gone, the Wheeldon children were left to make

their own way once more. On 1 June 1920 Hettie Wheeldon and Arthur McManus were married at Brentford Register Office. Hettie, now calling herself 'Harriette', was working as a shop assistant and her address appears on her marriage certificate as 29 Windmill Road, Chiswick. McManus was employed as an engineer, but listed his address as 907 London Road, Derby – Alice's old house. Winnie served as one of the witnesses. The couple set up home at 1 Beddington Terrace, Mitcham Road, Croydon, but it was to be a short and tragic marriage. Just five months after their wedding, on 29 October, Hettie gave birth prematurely to a daughter. The following day the ailing baby, named Sonya, died, the unsophisticated medical care of 1920 insufficient to sustain her tiny life. Three days later Arthur went to the local register office to record his daughter's birth. An E.L. Finn, perhaps a family friend or nurse, who had been present, registered the baby's death. There was more tragedy to follow. On 10 November Hettie became ill with appendicitis. She died three days later of heart failure, weakened by an operation to remove the troublesome organ. Her brother Will, who had been living with his sister and brother-in-law, was at her bedside and it was he who registered her death.

Will Wheeldon belonged to the Socialist Workers Party of England from June 1919 to July 1920 and was one of the first members of the Communist Party of Great Britain. Some accounts have suggested that he moved to Burton upon Trent and took a job at the local Co-op before marrying and raising a family, but this is inaccurate. According to the Passport Office, on 28 May 1921 Will Wheeldon was issued with a British passport. Shortly thereafter he travelled to Soviet Russia where he became a naturalised citizen. The Passport Office believed he had settled in Samara, an industrial city on the Volga. The city's arms, a white buck standing in a small grassy area beneath a coronet, is very reminiscent of Derby's own buck-in-the-park symbol. By 1927 he was well settled as a member of the All Union Communist Party. Between 21

December 1929 and 14 June 1937 he was employed as a translator by the Executive Committee of the Communist International (Comintern), which had been established to organise and promote the overthrow of the 'bourgeoisie' and the establishment of Communist governments across the world, as well as create a super-soviet state. Party records note that he was 'a good translator'.

Nellie Wheeldon, who had not been implicated in the alleged plot, now became more and more involved in politics. There are reports of her having married Tom Bell, but no records of such a union have been traced, and in 1931 Nellie boarded the SS *Albert Ballin* at Southampton. She disembarked at Cherbourg but the passenger manifest records that this was not her final destination. Her 'land of intended permanent residence' was listed as Russia. In all likelihood she intended to join her brother.

Will was a confirmed follower of Trotsky and held what Stalin and his followers considered 'Rightist tendencies'. His beliefs earned him a reprimand from the Communist Party. On 5 October 1937 Will Wheeldon was one of five members of the translations department arrested as Stalin continued his Great Purge against his political opponents. On 25 December the Military Board of the Supreme Court of the USSR sentenced him to be shot. It was probably some time before Nellie found out the truth of what had happened to her brother. Relatives of most of those imprisoned were told that their family members had been sentenced to ten years' imprisonment, during which time they would be unable to correspond with anybody. When the ten-year spells were over, the concerned families were informed that the prisoners had died some time earlier, with the dates and causes of deaths invented by the secret service.

The fate of Winnie and Alf Mason is far from clear. While they appear to have made a full recovery from pneumonia, there is little conclusive evidence of what happened to them after this. There have been suggestions that the couple, their marriage in tatters, emigrated together to Australia to rebuild their lives. Others suggest that the couple may have had a son, although this is unsubstantiated. In the *Derby Evening Telegraph* Lydia Robinson's granddaughter stated that Winnie had moved to South London, where she ran a dairy, and that Alf had encountered financial difficulties. What is known is that in February 1919 the couple had placed a notice in *The Socialist* thanking 'comrades and friends [for] numerous kindnesses and expressions of sympathy during the past two years and for the strenuous endeavours made on their behalf'. In 1928 the Passport Office received an application from Winnie to endorse her passport so that she could make a journey to Russia to visit her brother.

In May 1917 Arthur McManus and several other leaders of the National Committee of Shop Stewards were arrested. F.E. Smith was again the prosecutor. Tom Bell noted: 'It is doubtful if a more spiteful, hateful enemy of the workers ever existed . . . he blustered and threatened to send them to the front to be shot.' Eventually all the men were set free. In the General Election of 1918 McManus failed in a bid to become elected as a Labour MP in Halifax and soon became inspired by the Russian October Revolution to promote an international Communist Party.

In 1919 the SLP, of which he remained a prominent member, pulled out of talks to form a British Communist Party. McManus, Willie Paul and Tom Bell, working independently, continued negotiations and in April 1920 formed the Communist Unity Group which, in August that year, helped to form the Communist Party of Great Britain with McManus as its first chairman. He was later elected to the executive committee of Comintern. In 1925 McManus, along with Tom Bell and twenty-three other CPGB officials, was imprisoned after being found guilty of 'seditious libel and incitement to mutiny'. In early February 1927 he travelled to Brussels to attend the founding conference of the League Against Imperialism, which counted men such as Albert Einstein and

Jawaharlal Nehru among its active members. Arthur McManus died in London at the Royal Free Hospital on 27 February 1927, another victim of influenza. In recognition of his work his remains were interred in the Kremlin Wall Necropolis.

The Wheeldons' close friend Willie Paul remained resident in Derby for the rest of his life. Like McManus, Paul had unsuccessfully stood for Parliament in 1918, this time for Wigan. Undeterred, he stood again in the General Elections of 1922 and 1924, for the constituency of Manchester Rusholme. Ironically, although he stood as a Communist, the local Labour Party supported his candidacy. In 1921 Paul became editor of the *Communist Review*. He also edited the *Sunday Worker* and contributed to *The Communist* and *Labour Monthly*. During the 1930s and 1940s Paul was active in the Anglo-Soviet friendship movement and during the Second World War raised a great deal of aid for the Soviet allies. In the 1950s he was a supporter of the Derby Peace Council. Willie Paul died in March 1958, aged 73.

John S. Clarke became editor of *The Worker* and used its pages for repeated attacks on the use of agents provocateurs and against Alex Gordon in particular, reminding him that he had 'Alice Wheeldon's blood on his hands'. Following Gordon's return to Britain, and his interview in the *Daily Herald*, Clarke issued another verbal assault. Shortly thereafter Clarke received a letter from Gordon. Dated 6 February 1920, it read: 'Sir, I have noted your filthy and criminal libels. Rest assured you will shortly have the chance of answering them, Alex Gordon, Southampton.' Clarke was little troubled by this and published it in *The Worker* under the heading 'Another Night's Sleep Lost'. After his verbal tussle with Alex Gordon, Clarke continued to preach the word of Socialism. He lectured extensively on Marxism, but did not join his former comrades in the CPGB because he was uncomfortable with their enthusiastic adherence to everything dictated by Moscow. In 1929 he was elected Labour MP for Glasgow Maryhill, where he served for two years. In October 1931 he narrowly escaped death when he decided against a planned flight on the *R101* airship. The dirigible crashed, killing forty-eight of the fifty-four people on board. Clarke later worked as a journalist and served on Glasgow City Council for fifteen years before his death in 1947.

Little is known of the fate of the Wheeldons' barrister, Saiyid Haidan Riza. On 28 April 1922 he left his home in Loraine Road, Holloway, to board the Orient liner *Ormonde*, bound for Colombo in Ceylon (Sri Lanka). The passenger manifest lists his eventual permanent residence as India. He was travelling alone.

Riza's adversary, F.E. Smith, became Baron Birkenhead in 1919 and was appointed Lord Chancellor by Lloyd George. He enjoyed a good relationship with the Irish republicans Arthur Griffith and Michael Collins and helped establish the Irish Free State in 1922, an achievement which many believe somewhat thwarted his political ambitions. He was made Earl of Birkenhead the same year. He was out of government during the Bonar Law administration and during this period was publicly insulting and patronising towards his opponents. Under Stanley Baldwin he became Secretary of State for India but rumours of drunkenness proliferated and it is thought that this ended his political career. He wrote a number of books, one of which contained a colourful account of the Wheeldon affair, in which his memory of the case seemed to have faded. He died in London in 1930.

It is thought that Major Melville Lee retired from the secret service when his department was closed down, but retained some links with MI5. He established and edited a journal entitled *Industrial Peace* in which he circulated information about left-wing individuals and organisations.

Frederick De Valda remained in the intelligence services until the end of the war. He travelled the globe and dabbled in business and innovation. He began lecturing in schools with the aid of a film projector and wrote a series of adventure and fantasy novels. In 1933 his autobiography *Full Measure* was published. It features a highly embellished account of the Wheeldon case. Curiously, claiming that the Official Secrets Act required him to disguise the names of those involved, De Valda altered the Wheeldons to the Wheelers while the Masons became the Taylors, although their addresses and other identifying details remained unaltered. Like many of those who wrote a personal account of the case, De Valda slanted the 'facts' in order to highlight his own involvement.

Sir Frederick Low, the Old Bailey judge, died soon after the trial, in early September 1917, aged 60.

Bernard Spilsbury, the prosecution's star scientific witness, was knighted in 1923. Ultimately, Spilsbury would enjoy an extraordinary career, during which he would be involved in nearly every major murder trial in the south of England. He would play an important role, too, in the investigation into the *R101* airship disaster, and participated in Operation Mincemeat during the Second World War, an operation made famous in the film *The Man Who Never Was*. Spilsbury was responsible for a great many advances in forensics, including the importance of blood-spatter patterns. Through his work with the General Medical Council he promoted forensic science and established several university forensic medical courses. In 1935 he oversaw the founding of the police scientific department at Hendon and several Home Office laboratories. Spilsbury sought solace from life's tragedies (a broken marriage, the death of his sister and two of his sons) in his work, despite crippling arthritis. In December 1947 he committed suicide by carbon monoxide poisoning in his laboratory.

Sir Basil Thomson, commander of Special Branch, continued to control British Intelligence throughout the First World War until MI5 took over this role. He retired in 1921 and remained a well-respected national hero until an incident in 1925 when he was arrested in Hyde Park, having 'misconducted' himself with a young woman, Thelma de Lava. She was, it seemed, a prostitute, or 'actress' as she preferred to describe herself.

According to one newspaper report, the policeman who had arrested Thomson told Marlborough Police Court that Sir Basil 'was violating public decency . . . sitting on a park bench with his arms around the woman's neck . . . and all that'. After identifying himself to the young bobby, Thomson had apparently offered to 'make it possible for you to leave the force tomorrow', if he could overlook the misdeed.

Sir Basil claimed that he had been researching a book and had only

> gone to Hyde Park to gather data at first hand . . . As I entered the park I was accosted by a young woman, and we sat down upon two chairs placed under a tree at some distance from the public walk . . . when she said she was hard up, I unbuttoned my coat for the purpose of getting out a few shillings and giving them to her . . . At that moment the police officer . . . fairly charged down upon us.

Thomson was able to call upon some high-profile character witnesses, the Rt Hon Reginald McKenna, a former Home Secretary and the alleged victim of Alice Wheeldon's 'poisoned-needle-in-a-skull' plot among them. Two other witnesses stated that Thomson had often mentioned going to Hyde Park for the purposes of research. Despite his advocate's assertion that he was one of 'the greatest criminologists in England' and that it had been far too dark at the time for anyone to have seen anything that might or might not have been happening, Sir Basil was found guilty and fined £5 and costs amounting to an equal sum. Despite his claims of a malicious prosecution by his enemies and an official appeal, Sir Basil's reputation was forever tainted.

David Lloyd George continued as Prime Minister following the 1918 General Election, although he relied upon the support of the Conservatives who opposed his radical social reforms. He attended the Paris Peace Conference that drafted the Treaty of Versailles. In 1922 he was involved in a scandal that involved the awarding of knighthoods and peerages in exchange for money. In October 1922 the Conservatives, afraid that he might go to war with Turkey, ousted him. Throughout his life Lloyd George remained an advocate of social change. In 1936 he met Adolf Hitler in an attempt to dissuade the Führer from further military activity. In 1944 David Lloyd George was made an earl. He died in March 1945.

Arthur Henderson, the other proposed victim of the plot, about whom so little was made during the trial, served under Ramsay MacDonald as Home Secretary from 1923 and Foreign Secretary from 1929. In the latter role he established diplomatic relations with the USSR and supported the League of Nations. In 1931 he lost his parliamentary seat at Burnley, but was re-elected two years later as the member for Clay Cross in Derbyshire. Between 1932 and 1935 he chaired the Geneva Disarmament Conference, and was awarded the Nobel Peace Prize in 1934. He died, aged 72, in 1935.

Herbert Booth and Alex Gordon disappeared from view after the trial, in Gordon's case perhaps metamorphosing into one of his aliases. After his threatening letter to John S. Clarke, he apparently decided against legal proceedings, or had the decision made for him. Some accounts suggest that Booth may have died in King's Cross around 1950. Others claim that Gordon was eventually committed to a mental asylum. They simply faded into history.

Epilogue

The trial of Alice and Hettie Wheeldon and Alf and Winnie
Mason left many unanswered questions about the supposed
plot to kill David Lloyd George. The most pressing of these, of
course, is whether there was a plot at all. But without the
future unearthing of a hitherto undiscovered confession from
a Wheeldon or Mason, or even from Alex Gordon, this is likely
to remain unanswered. It is, though, perhaps possible to
consider whether today, with the same evidence available, a
case would be brought at all. Certainly the method employed
by the secret service for gathering intelligence was unsophisticated. The use of paid, untrained and unregulated
informants meant that much of the evidence was unreliable.
In the Wheeldons' case the evidence was largely circumstantial. There was little to prove that they intended to
murder the Prime Minister, save the word of a government-
paid agent and the reports of another deemed so unreliable
that he was not even called as a public witness. The defendants' intercepted letters, while certainly inflammatory in
parts, were largely littered with everyday references, a peculiar combination of domestic and mundane chit-chat:
mother–daughter discussions about erratic menstrual cycles;

boasts of bargain buys at the sales; discussions about the weather; and news about their friends and allies as well as acquaintances more keen to support the war. Alone these offered no proof of a plot to kill the Prime Minister, only an intention to destroy internment camp guard dogs. By modern standards the case for the prosecution seems weak. But then there is little to be gained from using twenty-first-century hindsight. These protagonists lived in a very different Britain – a Britain of insecurity and fear, mired in a terrible, destructive war. Against this background, there was a rising tide of Socialism and an increasingly vocal anti-establishment movement. The initial gung-ho popularity of the war had begun to wane. The reality of horribly wounded, mentally injured young men returning home to loved ones in towns and villages previously oblivious to anything other than patriotism was beginning to change public opinion. Even those naturally predisposed to supporting the authorities were starting to question their country's involvement in a war that seemed, geographically at least, so distant.

Certainly, given the nature of the case against the Wheeldons, the authorities had little choice but to pursue an investigation. Accusations had been made via well-established channels, the family's correspondence clearly indicated some element of secrecy, and phials of poison had been discovered. Despite the authorities' concern over Gordon's reliability, and their eventual decision to omit his testimony, they had little choice but to take his allegations seriously. Had they not acted, and an attempt on Lloyd George's life been made, the consequences would have been unthinkable.

There were other deciding factors, too. Once the suspects were arrested and the story had broken, it would have proved highly embarrassing to have to reverse course. In his later account of the case, F.E. Smith discussed the difficulties of taking the decision to prosecute: 'To commence a prosecution and then withdraw it inevitably causes a loss of prestige which may have disastrous consequences.' In other words, once they had acted on their suspicions, the authorities felt obliged to continue, with or without the evidence of Alex Gordon.

But might there have been a political reason for pursuing the Wheeldons? Might there even have been a motive to frame them, as some commentators have suggested? It is certainly possible that those in command of the intelligence agencies turned a blind eye to their agents' tendencies to exaggerate alleged plots. Is it then possible that they tacitly accepted their tendencies to invent them? Or even that they actively encouraged this?

F.E. Smith was keen to point out that the 'conspirators had no encouragement or assistance from the enemy', but many accounts on the other side of the political spectrum assert that they did receive such from two agents of the very government they were supposedly plotting to overthrow; that the so-called conspiracy was entirely the construct of an unreliable, possibly unstable individual, hungry for reward or recognition. Or even that it was the invention of the security service itself, working for a government anxious to discredit the Socialist and pacifist movements. The Wheeldons were vocally opposed to the war, the government and the status quo and their opinions were well known in their home town. To have so-called pacifists accused of trying to murder the Prime Minister, politically active women taking on extremist causes, and Socialists effectively attempting to overthrow an elected government would surely only boost mistrust of the radicals and support for the authorities. Actively discrediting opponents is one of the oldest political tricks in the book.

And then we must consider the motivation of the jury. Even the best-intentioned jurors come into any case predisposed to their own political and moral beliefs and have their own bugbears and experiences to draw upon. At the Wheeldon trial they heard two accounts of the truth. One, from a government agent, alleged a terrible conspiracy against one of the best-loved men in the country. It suggested that radical individuals, intent on harming the war effort, had plotted to assassinate the Prime Minister. The other claimed that four pacifists, who readily admitted radicalism, wanted to remove the threat of guard dogs at an internment camp so that incarcerated conscientious objectors could be freed.

The result was unsurprising. By their own admission the defendants had been plotting illegal, subversive activity. The jurors knew nothing of the recruitment of government agents, or of Gordon's instability. They were shown only the convincing and affable Booth. Most likely they knew little of the world that the Wheeldons occupied, a world of radicalism and activism, and they might easily have been dazzled by the prosecution's array of famous advocates and expert witnesses. The jurymen had to weigh one account against the other. It was a matter of trust and mistrust. In the event they found no reason to disbelieve their government, and every reason to mistrust the Socialist radicals.

Although the main protagonists have long since gone to their graves, rumour, supposition and inaccuracy about the Wheeldon case continue to proliferate. Men like F.E. Smith and Sir Basil Thomson embellished their own accounts of the case, enhancing their roles along the way, and as lofty an institution as the Metropolitan Police added its own, probably unintentional, fiction by noting on the official website history of Special Branch that the Suffragettes were 'finally defeated following the discovery of a conspiracy to assassinate the Prime Minister by the use of a poisoned blow-dart'.

It is perhaps hardly surprising that the facts are hard to come by. For decades it was nigh on impossible to get anyone connected with the Wheeldons to talk about the case, local journalists' attempts being repeatedly blocked by a wall of silence. Their former neighbours were unwilling to associate themselves with such criminals; their allies were afraid of exposing themselves to the authorities. That the Wheeldons were guilty of something is in no doubt. The crimes they did admit to planning – the poisoning of guard dogs and assisting conscientious objectors to escape the country – were serious enough to warrant the use of secret codes to escape detection. More than ninety years on, whether they also concealed something much more sinister remains unresolved.

Principal Sources

Books

Bell, Thomas, *Pioneering Days* (London, Lawrence & Wishart, 1941)

Birkenhead, Earl of, *Famous Trials of History* (London, Hutchinson, 1926)

Challinor, Raymond, *John S. Clarke: Parliamentarian, Poet, Lion-tamer* (London, Pluto Press, 1977)

Craven, Maxwell, *Derby: An Illustrated History* (Derby, Breedon Books, 1988)

De Valda, Frederick, *Full Measure: The Chronicles of a Restless Soul* (London, Arthur Barker, 1933)

Marreco, Anne, *The Rebel Countess: The Life and Times of Constance Markiewicz* (London, Corgi, 1969)

Rippon, Nicola, *Derby Our City* (Derby, Breedon Books, 2002)

Rippon, Nicola, *Derbyshire's Own* (Stroud, Sutton Publishing, 2006)

Rowbotham, Sheila, *Friends of Alice Wheeldon* (London, Pluto Press, 1986)

Strutt, Lt.-Col. G.A., *The Derbyshire Yeomanry War History 1914–1919* fascimile edn (Uckfield, Naval & Military Press, 2005)

Thomson, Sir Basil, KCB, *The Story of Scotland Yard* (London, Grayson & Grayson, 1935)
Derby & District Directory 1915–1916

Newspapers
Daily Herald
Daily Mail
Derby Daily Telegraph
Derby Evening Telegraph
Derby Mercury
New York Times
The Socialist
Workers' Dreadnought

Archives
Fabian Society
Glasgow Caledonia University
Glasgow Digital Library
Marxists.org
National Archives
Yale University

Academic Paper
Williams, Carl, 'The Policing of Political Belief in Great Britain 1914–1918' (London, London School of Economics & Political Science Collections, 2002)

Index